D0897975

THE BOMB AND THE COMPUTER

The Bomb and the Computer

WARGAMING FROM ANCIENT CHINESE
MAPBOARD TO ATOMIC COMPUTER

by Andrew Wilson

 DELACORTE PRESS / NEW YORK, N. Y.

CONTENTS

INTRODUCTION

ABOUT SIX MONTHS after the Cuban missile crisis, the London *Times* carried a story from Washington which read:

FIGHTING WORLD NUCLEAR
WAR BY COMPUTER

The Defence Department has just completed a war game on computers, which, according to reports, confirms the belief that the United States would prevail in total nuclear war. . . .

The war game, known as Simulation of Total Atomic Global Exchange (STAGE), is said to have taken nearly three years to prepare and five months to play. Electronic symbols representing missiles, bombers, decoys, interceptions and the like were recorded on magnetic tape, and the game was played by feeding punch cards with instructions into the machines.

Altogether 160,000 instructions were given, and the computers determined which strikes were successful and what losses suffered. The specific results are still being tabulated and will remain secret.

STAGE, the *Times* pointed out, was the second electronic game of its kind to be played. The first, completed three years before, had presumably been fought on the intelligence calculation, subsequently proved incorrect, that the Soviet Union had a preponderance of missiles. This had led to a rapid increase in the defense budget.

Anybody reading this must immediately have been struck by a number of questions. For example, how can a machine take account of fear, despair, and other human factors which must play a role in anything so cataclysmic as a nuclear war? Who designs and operates such machines? How much reliance is placed on them by governments? Are they used to predict the outcome of other events, such as wars to "pacify" Southeast Asia?

Such questions are the starting point of this book. But computer games are only one of the methods by which today's military planners seek answers to their often unanswerable questions. Their use can be explained only by reference to other methods such as Operations Analysis, Systems Analysis, and Game Theory, to which they are complementary. Moreover, the quest for certainty in military planning is not new. In the eighteenth century attempts were made to reduce the craft of war to a study of geometry, and in the early nineteenth to a question of railway timetables. To see modern war games in perspective it is necessary to observe earlier games, and the disasters to which they occasionally led. Again, one cannot describe the military use of war games without touching on the use of similar games for academic research in international relations and social science, as well as in business and for economic studies. Finally, computer games are used not merely to seek answers about today's and tomorrow's weapons systems, but also to generate "scenarios" about the possible shape of the world in general in ten, fifteen, and twenty years' time.

These aspects of operational research have led me further afield than my starting point might indicate. But in the end they all point to one question: Have we the intelligence to master the environment which weapons of mass destruction have created?

There is nothing academic about this question, however much the past twenty years may have fostered a feeling that nuclear deterrence "works." Although the Great Powers have managed to avoid a mutually annihilatory clash, they have not succeeded (even had they wished to) in eliminating sub-nuclear types of war. And so long as resort may be had to such war, the risks of escalation to nuclear war will remain. In fact they may be growing—for several reasons. Firstly, the threat of "automatic" escalation is now being explored as a means of cutting the financial burden of conventional forces, for example in Europe by the NATO Nuclear Affairs Committee. While this may look relatively safe in the present political climate, it could appear very different if that climate changed. Secondly, international violence has taken on a new respectability in recent years, exemplified by three major "limited" wars—in Vietnam, the Middle East, and the Indian subcontinent. Today such wars are partly restrained by the participants' lack of nuclear weapons or, as in Vietnam, by moral objections to their use. But cheap nuclear production processes will put nuclear weapons within physical reach of at least twelve more countries by 1980; and it requires only one small nuclear war to make nuclear war "respectable" also.

Thirdly, technological advances by the Great Powers themselves—in rocketry and counter-rocketry, orbital warhead delivery, deep-diving submersibles, chemical, and bacteriological weapons—now extend the opportunity for a new arms race of a qualitative nature potentially more destabilizing than the quantitative missile race of the 1960s. All this, plus the growing tensions caused by world hunger, poverty, and racism, may indeed soon cause us to look back at the 1960s as a decade of relative peace and security.

Now, the military planning techniques which this book describes may appear, in many cases, to have contributed to the dangers which I have mentioned. But it would belittle the nature of our present predicament to let pass the impression that war games are generally a pastime of men who take war lightly. On the contrary—and this is the heart of the matter—they are more often devised and played by serious technicians who, I have no reason to doubt, are personally as concerned to avoid the disaster of a major war as many people in the "peace movement."

The tragedy is that such techniques are directed to the attainment of impossible certainties about security and stability, while the very size of the effort devoted to them tends to foster the belief that they must succeed. At the same time research into alternative methods of promoting international security is left to a handful of "peace researchers" whose resources are paltry in relation to the size and urgency of their task. I do not believe that such alternative research can produce quick answers to the problem. But I do, as a military writer, find a curious imbalance in the effort we devote to planning for war as against the effort to discover and control its sources.

The size of the estabilshment involved in the production and use of what is called military "software" is indeed enormous. Though figures are hard to come by, I estimate that between 15,000 and 30,000 officers and scientists are concerned with war gaming of one kind or another at the present time, in America alone. About a quarter of them are directly employed by the Department of Defense. The rest are on the payrolls of aerospace and electronics corporations, or staff members of civilian "think tanks" which conduct military research on contract.

I owe several such institutions a considerable debt for help in preparing this book, and although I fear some may consider I have ill repaid it with the doubts I cast on their methods, I take this opportunity of thanking—and describing—them.

The largest and best known is the Rand Corporation at Santa Monica, California, which employs more than 1,100 people, half of them research scientists. Rand started as a research organization of the U.S. Air Force after World War II, was turned into an independent nonprofitmaking corporation in 1948. About 70 percent of its work is still performed for the Air Force on contract. The rest is mainly for the Office of the Secretary of Defense and the National Aeronautics and Space Administration, but a small percentage is "private research" undertaken at its own discretion from its own funds.

The Stanford Research Institute, another nonprofit organization, was founded in 1946 by a group of West Coast business leaders in cooperation with Stanford University. Based at Menlo Park, near San Francisco, its 1,400 professional staff members work mainly in the general scientific field, but it has major programs involving the use of war games in antiballistic missile defense, air defense, naval warfare, and unconventional warfare.

The Hudson Institute, at Croton-on-Hudson, near New York, is best known through its director, Herman Kahn, who has made extensive use of war games for gaining insights into "unthinkable" futures.

Among the universities the leader in defense research is the Massachusetts Institute of Technology, which has played a major role in developing politico-military games and computer simulations of guerrilla warfare problems. Harvard, close by, is the seat of Thomas Schelling, and Princeton that of Oskar Morgenstern—both pioneers of Game Theory.

Northwestern University, near Chicago, heads the field in computer games for the study of international relations—a social science activity as the university sees it, but "military social science" as the Defense establishment sees it (and supports it with funds from the Advanced Research Projects Agency).

Among the electronics and aerospace companies engaged in using or developing war games are the Raytheon Corporation, IBM, the Bendix Corporation, MacDonnell-Douglas, Lockheed, and Boeing; to whom must be added a number of firms and organizations primarily concerned with software production such as Technical Operations, Incorporated (who designed STAGE), Abt Associates, Inc., and the Research and Analysis Corporation (RAC).

Of the military war-gaming establishments the "senior" is the Joint War Games Agency of the Joint Chiefs of Staff. Its modest size (about 50 officers) is explained by the fact that for computers, game design, research into new techniques, and many administrative functions it draws on the vast resources of the National Military Command Systems Support Center of the Defense Communications Agency.

The U.S. Army is responsible for the Strategy and Tactics Analysis Group (STAG) at Bethesda, Maryland, with three big computers, a staff of 150, and a budget of $1,750,000 a year. Navy war gaming is under an Assistant for War Gaming Matters, responsible to the Chief of Naval Operations. From its center at Silver Spring, Maryland (part of the physics laboratory of Johns Hopkins University), there are links to computers in the old Washington Naval Yard, the naval Warfare Analysis Division at Norfolk, Virginia, and the Naval Warfare Center at the Pentagon.

The Marine Corps has a War Games Division at its Landing Force Development Center at Quantico, Virginia. But the Marines have a sturdy contempt for computers, use a minimum of electronic apparatus, and would really be happy to play war games with dice.

The U.S. Air Force, as we have seen, leans heavily on Rand.

In addition, all the Services use war games at their War Colleges; and there are war-gaming sections at numerous command headquarters at home and overseas, including Supreme Headquarters Allied Powers Europe (SHAPE) at Casteau in Belgium.

Although, for obvious reasons, I cannot name many of the individuals to whom I owe thanks for discussing current war-gaming matters, I must particularly thank Mr. Francis McHugh of the U.S. Naval War College for sharing with me his great knowledge of the historical aspect of war gaming in the United States. Also in the historical context I must thank Mr. M. W. Summerton of King's College, London, for directing me to sources of information about the great British war game of 1905; Mr. D. W. King, of the Ministry of Defence Library, London, for his kindness in locating numerous references to my subject; and the *Kriegsarchiv*, Vienna, for generous access to its material on Austrian and German games.

Finally, and not least, I must thank my wife, who first prompted me to try to explain what war gaming involves and whose knowledge of the subject stems from our co-translation, ten years ago, of Professor Gerhard Ritter's *Der Schlieffen Plan.*

This is not an "angry" book though, as the reader may discover, it is inevitably a rather pessimistic one. It will have served some purpose, however, if it encourages the reader to learn more about the nature of the military planning that is done in his name, and move writers, more expert than myself, to try to explain to the general public the problems and pitfalls of present-day Defense.

THE BOMB AND THE COMPUTER

1

THE PRUSSIAN
LEGACY

WHEN AND WHERE did war games start?

To this basic question there are half a dozen answers. Some would say with the Prussian *Kriegsspiel* of the early nineteenth century. Others with the invention of systems which preceded it by more than one hundred and fifty years. Sailors could point to the naval game invented by the Englishman John Clerk about 1790. But it is probably to ancient China, which also gave us gunpowder and the great military thinker Sun-Tzu, that we must credit the invention of simulating battle on a board.

The Chinese game Wei-Hai originated about 3000 B.C. in roughly the same form as that in which it is still played today under the Japanese name of Go. It was played on a stylized mapboard with different colored stones and won by the player who succeeded in outflanking his opponent. This was the principle of Sun-Tzu's teaching and also of the German generals who sought to envelop the armies of France in 1914. The Chinese name means simply "encirclement."

The other ancient forebear of the modern computer war game is Chaturanga, a Hindu game which also used a stylized map and whose pieces included foot soldiers, chariots, light cavalry, and elephants. It was played by four persons and the outcome of moves was determined by throwing dice. Some theorists have suggested that Chaturanga was evolved by pacifist Brahmans as a "moral equivalent" to war, a function sometimes attributed to chess, which began as a copy of it by Europeans. If so, it can only be observed that it signally failed to gain general acceptance as a substitute for the real thing.

Attempts have been made to find other origins of the modern war game, for example in the game of checkers of ancient Egypt and Mesopotamia. But the fact is that across the span of history embracing such great captains as Alexander, Scipio Africanus, Belisarius, Gustavus Adolphus, and Oliver Cromwell, there is little evidence that, outside China, games were ever used as a way to study military problems.

It was not until the Age of Reason, when men decided that the conduct of war, like other human pursuits, was subject to scientific laws, that games reappeared which consciously reproduced the elements of war for play. In the literature of strategy chess is sometimes cited as an example of a two-sided war game in which all moves were visible to both players. But except for a brief period it has remained without military pretensions.

The exception occurred in the seventeenth century when chess gave birth to a variety of chesslike games which reflected the military developments of a new age. Their pieces included not only Knights and Castles, but also pikemen, halberdiers, and the new light artillery invented by the English in the form of the longbow. In 1644 a Christopher Weikhmann, at Ulm, developed a war chess called the "King's Game." It had fourteen fixed moves and thirty pieces on each side, including the king, a marshal, two chaplains, and eight private soldiers. It is said to have been highly regarded as an aid in military training.

In the early eighteenth century two French games, *Le Jeu de la Guerre* and *Le Jeu de la Fortification,* made their appearance, dealing with open and siege warfare respectively. Instead of "men" they made use of cards and were used to familiarize students with basic military facts. Until the Second World War a set remained in the British War Office, a treasured acquisition of the Military Intelligence branch.

The belief that war was an exact science, and the quest for "true principles" to guide its conduct, soon led to the design of more complicated games. In 1780 Helwig, Master of Pages to the Duke of Brunswick, devised a game that for the first time used single pieces to represent whole military units rather than individual soldiers. Five kinds of terrain were represented and could be used to build up a battlefield divided into 1,666 squares. The various arms were given different movement rates, and provision made for an independent "director" to apply the game rules. The forces on each side included no less than

     60 battalions of Grenadiers
     25 battalions of Pontoniers
      8 squadrons of Dragoons
     10 squadrons of Hussars
     10 batteries of Field Artillery
      3 batteries of Siege Artillery
      2 batteries of Mortars.

The most elaborate game of this type was achieved about 1800 in the so-called *Neues Kriegsspiel* of Viturinus, which had sixty pages of rules and was played on 3,600 squares depicting actual terrain on the Franco-Belgian border. The troop lists ran to 1,800 brigades (a third of them cavalry), 600 batteries of field artillery, and 200 batteries of horse artillery. Reinforcements and logistical units were introduced as necessary. The forces thus assembled exceeded the numbers which were to be locked in battle on the Western Front more than a century later, and it is hardly surprising that Viturinus' complicated rules made it impossible to maneuver in the end.

It might be thought that the shock of Napoleon's victories, which owed nothing to pseudomathematical science, would have led to a decline of interest in the more elaborate type of war game, as it did to the "mathematical" outlook among European generals. But in Germany the urge to game war proved irrepressible. In 1809 a further refinement of military chess was invented by the son of a Dresden artist, Schnorr von Carolsfeld, who introduced it to the Saxon court. Three Saxon princes—Anton, August, and Johann—were present at these games and remembered them later as a pleasant diversion in a time of trouble. But the real nursery of the war game, professionally played, was the court of Prussia.

In 1811 the young Prussian princes Frederick and William heard from their tutor that a war game had been invented by a Herr von Reisswitz, living in Berlin. Reisswitz was invited to the palace and given a room for his apparatus, which consisted of a plaster relief model representing a large stretch of country on a scale of twenty-six inches to the mile. The troops were represented by small blocks of wood stuck with colored paper and were moved according to the inventor's rules.

The boys told the King about the game, and a year later Reisswitz presented him with an improved model and a set of porcelain pieces. From then on the King became an addict and used to sit up long after his usual bedtime to finish games with the Prince of Mecklenburg. From this touching domestic beginning the war game spread to Russia; for Prince William, who on these occasions acted as the King's assistant, developed a passion for it and in 1816 and 1817 played it with the Czarevitch Nicholas during visits between Berlin and Moscow.

Meanwhile a development took place in the game itself, when Reisswitz' invention was taken over by his son, a lieutenant of the artillery. Substituting a large-scale map (about eight inches to the mile) for the relief model, the younger Reisswitz developed the rules into a system more closely resembling the real conditions of war. He introduced metal pieces, in scale with the map, to represent infantry, cavalry and artillery units, coloring one army red and the other blue —a convention which persists to this day. The game was played by two-minute moves during which each commander was allowed to move any or all of his pieces a distance compatible with that which real troops could have covered in the time. Disputes were settled by an umpire, who also decided the result of each engagement, with dice and a code of rules.

The die was introduced to represent the element of chance in war. When a decision was required, the umpire would estimate the chances of each side, according to its strength. On this estimate he would assign each side a number of faces on the die, or rather select a die with the appropriate proportion of red and blue sides. For example, if Blue, with 200 men, attacked Red, with 100 men, Blue's chances were taken as two to one and a die selected with four blue faces and two red. The second stage was to settle how many men on each side had been put out of action. For this there was a table showing the losses of any given force under various conditions, according to estimates derived from a study of military history.

In 1819 Lieutenant Reisswitz was transferred from Stettin to Berlin, where he set about perfecting his system. His chief associates were four fellow subalterns—von Greisheim, von Herwarth, von Vincke, and von Dannhauer—three of whom were to become Prussian generals. Early in 1824 Reisswitz and his friends were asked to explain their system to Prince William, now commander of a Guards division. A lecture by Reisswitz, and a game between the Prince and Dannhauer, led to the performance being repeated before the General Staff. The Chief of the Staff, General Karl von Müffling, is said to have received the players rather coldly at first

> . . . but as the operations expanded on the map, and move by move the combatants worked out their plans, the old general's face lit up, and at last he broke out with enthusiasm: "It's not a *game* at all, it's training for war. I shall recommend it enthusiastically to the whole army." [1]

A few days later a notice of Müffling's approval appeared in the *Militär Wochenblatt,* and a royal order was given to every regiment to procure the apparatus and charge the expense to its budget.

This was the beginning of the *Kriegsspiel* as a serious military pursuit, which was to spread to almost every country with military pretensions. Prince William wrote to his old playmate the Czarevitch, who promptly asked not only for a set of the apparatus but also for its inventor. Reisswitz was sent to St. Petersburg and spent a summer at Prince Nicholas' palace. Prince Nicholas then spent a winter in Berlin and fought a regular campaign against Prince William with Müffling and Reisswitz acting as umpires. Later the same year (1825) Marshal Marmont, on his way from Paris to St. Petersburg, attended a game and spoke highly of its instructional value.

In Berlin itself, perhaps under pressure of the royal edict, the war game became immediately fashionable, and among its addicts in 1828 was Lieutenant Helmuth von Moltke, then a member of the Topographical Bureau. Various societies were formed to play it, including the Berlin *Kriegsspieler Verein* which published a handbook in 1846. By 1874 there were seven such societies in the Military Academy alone. Among the favorite umpires were such famous Prussian tactical writers as von Verdy du Vernois, von Meckel, and von Scherff.

---

[1] S. Wilkinson, *Essays on the War Game* (London, 1887).

From Berlin the game also spread to Turkey. For when Captain Moltke was presented to the Ottoman commander, Chosref Pasha, at Constantinople, one of the old man's first questions was about the use of war-game maps and men, of which he possessed a set. Ten years later Moltke, still a keen war gamer, became chief of the 4th Army Corps at Magdeburg, where he was soon surrounded by an enthusiastic circle of *Kriegsspiel* players. Another *Kriegsspiel* center was Königsberg, headquarters of the 1st Army Corps, whose society possessed a series of ingenious maps given it by General Dannhauer, Reisswitz' early companion. It was also at Königsberg that General von Verdy du Vernois perfected his system. Two other centers deserve mention: Neisse, the home of the so-called Tschischwitz code, from which the British war game rules were translated, and Dresden, where a young officer, Captain Naumann, introduced a system which was to capture the attention of a British Major Kitchener.

But from all these glories one spectator was missing. In 1826 poor Reisswitz, on being promoted captain, had been transferred from Berlin to Torgau in Saxony. The move, says his chronicler, "took him away from his friends and placed him in a circle where neither he nor his game were appreciated. His sensitive nature fell prey to despondency, and next year, on leave of absence, he shot himself." [2]

Lamented though it was by a generation of Prussian officers, his death saved Reisswitz from seeing his game drastically changed in their hands. Its essence had been the rigidity of its rules. But when it came to be played by tacticians this rigidity was bound to be questioned. Not only did the outcome of engagements often seem to contradict tactical sense, but the umpire was reduced to being a mere calculator. So long as the Prussian army was still learning its trade, officers lacked battle experience. But the wars against Austria (1866) and France (1870) changed this.

2 *Ibid.*

Von Meckel, writing in 1874, puts it nicely. It was not, he says, that Reisswitz lacked tactical sense, but that the sense became buried in the rules. Umpires tended to give decisions based on the rules rather than on tactical reality. As a result, despite the orders of the All Highest, the game did not gain universal acceptance. "It led more the life of a hot house plant" and even when more practical considerations gained ground, its enemies were always more numerous than its friends. "If after the wars of 1866 and 1870, the game enjoyed an upsurge, it was not due to the rules but rather in spite of them. It is doubtful if there was a single war game in the Prussian Army that was played according to the rules." [3]

One of the first things to go was the dice—their use, says von Meckel, "became generally superseded." For although dice could be useful in confronting officers with the unexpected, such as the death of a commander or a "bad day" for one side, judgments given by an umpire were better because "success and criticism could be matched."

Due to such changes there grew up, after 1870, a formal distinction between "free" and "rigid" *Kriegsspiel*. The latter, having detailed rules, was reserved for low-echelon tactical games (around which it produced a whole literature, often of great ingenuity) [4] while the former, in which events were judged at the umpire's discretion, became general for higher level games. This was so not only in the German but in all major European armies, on whose conduct in 1914 the use of war games was in some cases to have disastrous effects.

In the British Army the development of the *Kriegsspiel* went officially unnoticed for half a century. Then belatedly

---

[3] von Meckel, *Anleitung zum Kriegsspiel* (Berlin, 1875).
[4] One of the most ingenious games was devised by a Swedish Captain de Ridderstad. His *taktiska reliefkrigsspel* was played on eight square relief map sections. However arranged, each side of every square matched each side of every other square, providing several thousand combinations of imaginary territory. See *Le Jeu de la Guerre, en Relief*, by W. de Ridderstad, Stockholm, Imprimerie Centrale, 1886.

the Army decided to copy it. In this it may have been spurred not only by the cult of Prussian military methods which followed the Prussian victories of 1870, but also by the claim of Prussian officers such as Adolf von Trotha that war games had made an important contribution to their earlier successes. Characteristically the British authorities picked on the very "rigid" Neisse game of von Tschischwitz, which in Germany was already regarded as obsolete. The official British *Rules for the Conduct of the War Game* were published in 1872, and for the next twenty years a handful of British officers resorted to translating more recent German codes in an attempt to inject some vitality into the game.

The more ardent of these enthusiasts were to be found among the Volunteers—the remarkable force of amateur soldiers which had originally been raised to defend the kingdom during the French invasion scare of 1859—and the greatest of them all was the military reformer Spenser Wilkinson (1853–1937).

Wilkinson's historic contribution to British military history was to secure British interest in, and finally adoption of, the German General Staff system. His major literary work, *The Brain of an Army,* excited Moltke's exclamation that it should have been left to an Englishman to produce such a work. It was almost as a by-product of this interest that he became the foremost exponent of the war game in lectures to Volunteers.

Wilkinson entered the military world entirely by chance. The son of a Liberal and pacifist banker, he fortuitously acquired a sound schooling in German which took him in 1873 on a postgraduate scholarship to Merton College, Oxford. Touring Germany on his first vacation he happened to pick up an Austrian pamphlet comparing the strength of the armies of Europe. So shocked was he to discover the insignificance of the British army that he borrowed and read two military classics, Hamley's *Operations of War* and the recent Wellington Prize essay of Lieutenant (later General Sir John)

Maurice, *The System of Field Manœuvres Best Adapted for Enabling Our Troops to Meet a Continental Army*. Next term at Oxford he joined the Volunteer Corps and also set about organizing the Oxford Kriegsspiel Club.

In 1880 Wilkinson was called to the bar and started to practice in Manchester, where he had already taken a commission in the 2nd Manchester Volunteers. Shocked at the standard of military teaching in the regiment, he joined with six other enthusiasts in forming the Manchester Tactical Society. In the word of a recent study [5] this was the end of his legal career. "He continued to practice law, but his happiest hours were those spent with friends discussing war games and tactical problems. There developed a camaraderie rarely seen among volunteer organizations, and by a frank discussion of their blunders, a demanding program of reading and study, and rigorous self-examination they learned a great deal about the practical aspects of war."

The Manchester Tactical Society soon became a publishing fund which for many years was to put out Wilkinson's translations of French and German military texts, including the German Order of Field Service (1893), which was adopted by the War Office and which Wilkinson called "perhaps the most valuable book on the details of war that has ever been published." But for students of the *Kriegsspiel* Wilkinson's most interesting publication was *Essays on the War Game* consisting mainly of lectures to Volunteer officers and articles written for the *Manchester Guardian* (of which he was also dramatic critic).

In one of the *Essays* Wilkinson inquires into the nature of war games. "Probably no form of military study is more useful if properly conducted, as certainly none is so liable to be misused," he writes—a caution that has lost none of its validity today. Strictly speaking, he says, war games are maneuvers

[5] J. Luvaas, *The Education of an Army* (Chicago: University of Chicago, 1964; London: Cassell, 1965).

on a map. In short, they are a substitute for maneuvers with troops—a training which "like war itself, is too costly to be attainable except on rare occasions."

A crucial aid to this development had, of course, been the progress of map makers who were now, for the first time, capable of producing 1:5,000 and 1:10,000 scale sheets. As a result, "the officer to whom a good map speaks clearly requires nothing but a strong imagination to see armies maneuvering on the country which it represents. He can moreover assist his imagination by placing on the map bits of wood or metal cut so as to occupy on the map just so much country as would in reality be occupied by bodies of troops."

But there are pitfalls in such exercises, says Wilkinson. Unless an officer is thoroughly at home on a map, he can conduct his troops "no better than a blind general." Moreover the map must represent all the features that would be of importance to troops in action; otherwise it will never be more than a *sham* sham fight.

The *Essays* are full of homely advice on how to conduct a war game; of warnings against unrealistic "situations" and umpires who usurp the players' discretion. Weekend soldiers who take it on themselves to invent situations must be familiar "not only with the principles of strategy but with its machinery." Wilkinson prescribes them an impressive diet of reading: Jomini, Clausewitz, Blume, Hamley—"to be supplemented by some acquaintance with the details of army management from, say, Bronsart von Schellendorf's *Duties of the General Staff.*"

Having urged that war games should not be directed by anyone less than a keen student of battles (or better, an officer who could say "I saw an advance like this at the battle of Gravelotte"), Wilkinson comes to the *method* of conducting a game. Here, as might be expected, he directs readers to the extensive literature of Germany and Austria—"Too little is known in England." The official British rules, though revised in 1884, are still unsatisfactory. He recommends General von Verdy du Vernois, "the ablest writer who ever dealt with war games," who refused to be bound by rules altogether.

What is the usefulness of war games?—not any information acquired from them, but the test they present to combatants of tactical and strategical knowledge. "The only difference from actual war is the absence of danger, of fatigue, of responsibility, and of the friction involved in maintaining discipline." Of course, says Wilkinson, these factors are all-important in war. But since they are unmeasurable, in map maneuvers they are assumed to be equal on both sides. "The question therefore becomes—How many men must be killed or wounded before the remainder will be induced to change their mind and go back?"

On this he refers readers to the researches of the Saxon officer, Captain Naumann, whose rules or "tables" came to play a major part in European and American war-gaming. Naumann's rules were published in a pamphlet, *Das Regiments-Kriegsspiel,* in Berlin in 1877 and were based on a close study of the war of 1870. From this he concluded that the effect of losses on a unit varied according to conditions being "favorable" or "unfavorable." Favorable conditions occurred when the unit was attacking, i.e., was on the side which had been most successful in the war, or when its losses were spread over an hour or more in time. Unfavorable conditions were when it was on the long-term defensive, or when its losses were concentrated. Thus, under Naumann's rules a company of 250 German regulars could, in favorable circumstances, lose forty men without flinching, and would not be considered severely shaken until it had lost ninety. In *un*favorable circumstances it would be considered severely shaken when it had lost only sixty. A loss of 120, even in the most favorable circumstances, put a company "out of action," and a loss of 150 men was equivalent to its destruction.[6]

6 Naumann, *Das Regiments-Kriegsspiel* (Berlin, 1877. 2nd edition revised 1881).

Wilkinson recommends pasting Naumann's scale, adjusted to various ranges for rifle and artillery fire, on a foot rule for quick application to the map. At the same time he ridicules the 1884 rules by reference to an imaginary war-game charge in which one side—"under the influence, say, of some special correspondent's account of a Bulgarian charge at Slivnitza"— advances on the other's defensive fire without deigning to fire a shot. Under the rules, which lacked all Naumann's subtle- ties, the side making the charge could lose a third of its men "without so much as pausing or going to ground," and then stand an even chance of success in the subsequent hand-to- hand fighting, depending on the throw of the dice.

The reader who wishes to know what really happens in such circumstances, says Wilkinson, will do well to read the terrible account of the infantry brigade brought up by the Prussians in the afternoon on their left wing at Mars-la-Tour.

In due course Wilkinson's energy and abilities fixed on other tasks—reporting and criticizing the conduct of the war in South Africa, membership of the Royal Commission which gave existence to the Territorial Army, finally a Chichele pro- fessorship in military history at Oxford. The legacy of his war-game teaching may perhaps be detected in the great strategic war game of 1905, which we shall encounter later on. But at lower levels his tactical ideas had only partial suc- cess. Even keen Volunteer officers may have felt that he put his standards of instruction unnecessarily high. As for the Regular Army, although the library shelves of the old War Office contain a number of ingenious British war games—for example Major F. W. Kitchener's,[7] which uses a screen with peepholes for observation by cavalry scouts—one cannot help feeling that, once the Prussian vogue had been superseded by the Anglo-French Entente, the tactical war game was regarded as altogether too Germanic for the serious consideration of gentlemen.

[7] F. W. Kitchener, *Rules for War Games on Maps and Tactical Models* (Simla: Government Central Printing Office, 1895).

There were, however, no such inhibitions in the United States Army where, as in the British, the earliest war games began as copies or adaptations of the *Kriegsspiel*.

The first and most widely read American authority, Major W. R. Livermore, learned about war gaming from a civil engineer who had served with the Bavarian Army. Livermore's book, *The American Kriegsspiel,* appeared in 1879. The preface to the first edition says the author had consulted the works of von Tschischwitz, von Verdy, von Meckel, and von Trotha, but considered his work closest to the *Regiments-Kriegsspiel* of Naumann.

Livermore's rules were supposedly adaptable to five types of war game: Tactical, Grand Tactical, Strategical, Fortress, and Naval, though the naval application is not described. The game was played on a map which, in the case of tactical games, had ten-foot contours and a scale of twelve inches to the mile. Blocks were used in the German fashion, but there were numerous refinements intended to reduce the work of record keeping. For example, when a unit lost 20 percent of its fighting power the block was turned upside down to shown a "score mark"; when 40 percent was lost another face was turned up, and so on. Other devices showed the "gait" of a unit's march, the direction of fire, the degree of the troops' fatigue, and the extent of their disorganization after an action. The most elaborate device was a "firing board" on which losses were computed according to a system of points and "multipliers" based on German battle experience in the 1870 war.

In adapting the *Kriegsspiel* for American use Livermore, like others after him, faced a major problem: that the American army lacked firsthand experience of modern war. (He seems, like contemporary Europeans, to have underrated the lessons of the Civil War, in many ways more "modern" than those of the Franco-Prussian war.) This made impossible demands on the unaided judgment of American umpires. He therefore rejected the "free" type of war game while hoping that his improved equipment and procedures would "make the American game proceed almost as rapidly." But in this he was disappointed. For the time taken by players and umpires to master the firing board and other devices outweighed any timesaving in the game itself.[8] In a second edition of *The American Kriegsspiel,* published in 1898, he admits that although efforts have been made to bring the tables up to date, "we now have no recent war like the Franco-Prussian or Turco-Russian to test the value of our estimates"; and he goes on to caution umpires that his exact and comprehensive rules are only to be used "as required. . . . The computations not only *need* not, but *must* not, be made in every case."

Livermore's problem—how to devise a game suitable for small American garrisons—led a contemporary American officer, Lieutenant Charles A. L. Totten, to devise a rival game, or rather a set of games. Totten's games, which he called "Strategos," were intended "to blend and fade into one another so gradually and so naturally that the student will be almost unwittingly entrapped into continually higher and higher forms of study until at length the mere tyro . . . will find himself gradually venturing to command an army, and essay with growing confidence those deeper, and more absorbing, problems which test generalship and seal the fate of nations."

Totten, like Livermore, devised a Minor Tactical Game and a Grand Tactical Game, both of which were also called the Battle Game. Both resembled the old war chess, being played on a board forty-eight inches by forty inches divided into one-inch squares. The board was faced with slate so that notes could be written on it. The red and blue blocks representing units were also faced with slate for record-keeping purposes, and there were additional blocks to represent topographical features.

8 F. J. McHugh, "Fundamentals of War Gaming," 3rd edition (mimeo), Newport, R.I., U.S. Naval War College, 1966.

Pieces were moved according to rigid rules. An infantry unit could move one square forwards or sideways. Cavalry, rather like chess Knights, could move two squares diagonally and then one forwards, backwards, or sideways. Each piece had a numerical value and the rules governed capture and displacement of opposing forces. In the Grand Tactical Game, as in the British game of Kitchener, the players sometimes made their initial dispositions separated by a screen. The screen was then lifted for a short interval so that players might see, but not study, each other's dispositions. Subject to the umpire's approval, the players then adjusted their dispositions, the screen was lifted, and play began.[9]

Totten's "advanced game" was played on maps. Forces moved according to a table compiled from actual experience, their capability being modified by multipliers when conditions varied from the norm. Whether or not a unit could advance, hold its position, and so on was determined by ratios expressing chances of success. The actual outcome was then determined by throwing dice. For example, when veteran troops engaged raw troops, Totten doubled Caesar's odds and gave the veterans 4 to 1. Totten not only believed that this was realistic, but he also believed that the "chances of success" had a deep meaning in battle itself—a belief which, like his tables, was based on a painstaking study of War Department records of the Civil War. This, however, did not spare him the scorn of Livermore, who alleged that he had merely translated German texts.[10]

In the following years war gaming in America finally caught up with German developments, though neutrality mercifully precluded it from making a contribution to the disaster of 1914. The "free" game became widely adopted as a result of the translation, in 1897, of General von Verdy's book, under the American title *A Simplified Game of War;*

[9] J. G. Crowther and R. Whiddington, *Science and War* (London: HMSO, 1947).
[10] McHugh, *op. cit.*

and in 1908 Captain Farrand Sayre published *Map Manœuvres and Tactical Rides,* based on a series of lectures at the Army Staff College at Fort Leavenworth. Sayre introduced his students to the one-sided war game in which the umpire "played" the enemy forces. He also introduced the use of celluloid sheets, or overlays, which were placed over the maps in the game, and on which information and movements were drawn with colored wax pencils. With this, American Army war gaming acquired nearly all the technical devices which were to serve the art until after World War II. It would, however, be improper to end this chapter without reference to naval war games—a field in which the United States took an early lead.

The first device approximating to a naval war game was employed by an Englishman who never put to sea in his life. John Clerk's *An Essay on Naval Tactics,* embodying new principles of sea warfare, appeared towards the end of the eighteenth century and may have influenced Rodney in his action against de Grasse. In the preface Clerk explains that he worked out his theory with the help of "small models of ships which, when disposed in proper arrangement, gave most correct representations of hostile fleets." [11] After this a century elapsed before a Captain Philip Colomb of the Royal Navy invented a game called "The Duel." Patented by Colomb about 1878, the Duel was intended to simulate action between two opposing ships. Officers subsequently testified that it was "a capital game," "very useful," and that it afforded valuable information as to the tactics of gun and torpedo action.[12] But although it may have stimulated the playing of a similar game in the Russian Imperial Navy, it seems to have been more talked about than played in the British. At about the same time a naval war game called

[11] John Clerk, *An Essay on Naval Tactics* (Edinburgh: Constable, 1790).
[12] The British Whitehead torpedo, using a compressed air engine, was developed in 1886 from the concept of an Austrian naval officer, Giovanni Luppis.

"Manovra Sulla Carta" was invented by an Italian naval lieutenant with the hope that it would "form a useful and voluntary occupation." These two games were to become, in American hands, the inspiration of war studies of far-reaching effect.

The "father" of American naval war gaming was William McCarty Little, a naval lieutenant who came out of retirement in 1887 to deliver a series of six lectures on war games at the U.S. Naval War College at Newport. In the history of war games Little holds a position similar to Livermore in the United States and Spenser Wilkinson in Britain. For two years before his lectures he had worked at the College unofficially. In 1887 he was appointed to the staff and except for one short break remained there until his death in 1915. So large was his contribution to the development of American naval doctrine that in 1903 Congress, by a special act, appointed him to the rank of captain. However, at the time of Little's appointment there was little enthusiasm for theoretical pursuits in the U.S. Navy; and he and his war games would probably have gone unrecognized but for the interest of the then relatively unknown president of the College, Captain Alfred T. Mahan.

Initially the Newport war games were based partly on the British and Italian games, and partly on experience gained in games played by the staff. Notes were also exchanged with Livermore, who visited the College in 1889. Three types of games were conducted. The first, the duel, simulated action between two battleships armed with guns and torpedoes. The two players and an umpire used a sheet of paper spread out on a table. The rules provided data for scoring the effects of gunfire, torpedo fire, and ramming. Apart from instruction, the game was used to test the effects of variations in the turning radii of battleships and other parameters. But it was discontinued after 1905.

The second or tactical type of game, also known as the fleet or board game, represented action between opposing fleets of battleships and cruisers. It required six officers: two fleet commanders, a director or arbitrator, a recorder, and two movers. When land forts, destroyers, and submarines were involved, additional players were appointed to act as their commanders. The individual ships were represented by model sailing ships with red and blue hulls for the respective sides. Different colored sails were used to represent the various types of ships. Early tactical games were conducted on paper marked off into squares. Later wooden boards were used, and finally the squares were painted on the floor of the war game room. At the start of the game the ships were positioned in formation selected by the opposing commanders. The commanders prepared their orders in "signal book language" for each two-and-a-half-minute move. The game was stopped when the director considered it had achieved its purpose; but it could also be transferred to the scale of a duel game, when additional commanders would be assigned as commanders of individual ships. After 1893 tactical games were used to evaluate plans and doctrines. One factor thus investigated was the value of superior speed.

The third type of game, the strategic or "chart" game, was an altogether larger affair. Each comander-in-chief and his staff were assigned separate rooms, as were players who handled detached forces. The director compared the opposing sides' plans and selected a convenient length for the first move. When this was announced, the players plotted the movements of their forces and submitted the celluloid overlays to the control group, which plotted the tracks of the vessels on a master plot. When the opposing fleets came into battle range, the game was ended, or was transferred to the game board for continuation as a tactical game.

The degree to which war games shaped American naval plans before World War I was surpassed only by the influence of the *Kriegsspiel* on the plans of the German army. For many years, even after the turn of the century and the building of Alfred von Tirpitz' battle fleet, "Red" remained quaintly the British. Thus in 1894 games based on assumed hostilities between the United States and Britain led to a study of tactical defense plans for New England anchorages —a successful aid, as a contemporary issue of *Harper's Weekly* put it, to "complete preparedness against all probable contingencies." The following year games led the Naval War College to send a recommendation to the Navy for the construction of a Cape Cod canal.

In 1896, as the result of a war game, the College suggested experiments with fuel oil instead of coal; and in 1903 the playing of a strategic game showed the weakness of disseminated forces and caused the Navy to adopt the principle of concentration of the fleet. Three years later a game to examine the effect of various ship speeds was played no less than 120 times, and tactical games led to modifications of the current battle plan in the light of increased torpedo ranges. Not content with gaming its own problems, the Navy extended its activity to land war games and in 1911 evolved an elaborate coastal artillery game. Finally, on the eve of World War I games were used to demonstrate battle line tactics and the merits of the all-big-gun battleship.[13]

In naval war games such as those described it needs no special insight to see a difference from land war games. For the fighting ship is a creature of predictable capability, and although it remains under human control and subject to weather and other hazards, its performance can be convincingly simulated with the aid of mathematical instruments such as those used to direct it in action. Perhaps it is for this reason that—with a notable exception described in the next chapter—naval war games have generally inspired greater confidence than games intended to simulate other types of war.

[13] McHugh, *op. cit.*

2

FROM THE MARNE
TO MIDWAY

BEFORE THE FIRST WORLD WAR one of the greatest war
gamers was Alfred Graf Schlieffen, Chief of the German General Staff from 1892 to 1906. Not only did he personally
conduct innumerable games and "tactical rides," but the
whole "Schlieffen Plan" for the invasion of Belgium and
France was developed in accordance with war game "findings."

Schlieffen's character is recalled by a subordinate:

> For several years the bell of my flat would ring on Christmas Eve. A courier would bring his Christmas present: a
> great military exercise designed by himself for the set task of
> working out an operational plan. He would have been very
> surprised if the solution had not been in his hands on the
> evening of Christmas Day.

One year Schlieffen was traveling across East Prussia to the
great annual maneuvers at Insterburg.

In the morning the train left Königsberg and entered the Pregel valley, which was basking prettily in the rays of the rising sun. Up to then not a word had been spoken on the journey. Daringly his aide-de-camp tried to open a conversation and pointed to the pleasant scene. "An insignificant obstacle," said the Graf—and the conversational demands until Insterburg were therewith met.[1]

The Schlieffen Plan—more accurately a series of plans prepared between 1894 and 1905—was based on Schlieffen's professed conviction that sooner or later Germany would have to break out of her "encirclement" by France and Russia. Once he had decided to launch the attack against France first, the question was how to outflank the French main armies and frontier fortresses, stretching from Belgium to the Vosges. Schlieffen at first thought this could be done by a minor penetration of neutral Belgium south of the Meuse. But war games soon convinced him that to obtain enough room for the big force needed for the outflanking maneuver, it was necessary to pass through the whole of Belgium and perhaps part of Holland as well. By 1905 the maneuver became so extended that the troops of the right wing were to march within sight of the English Channel, sweep right around Paris, and fall on the French armies from the west.

Now, however, the problem was to find enough *men*. Schlieffen's first answer was to denude the German left wing in order to strengthen the right. But even when this was done, there were still barely enough troops to provide a margin over the French, let alone the Belgians (or the British, if they came to Belgium's help). His second answer, in 1905, was to create additional army corps from reservists. But even this was not enough, as his successor, the younger Moltke, found in 1914. It is now known that Schlieffen himself had grave doubts about the matter.[2] But instead of taking the honest course and warn-

[1] H. von Kuhl, *Der deutsche Generalstab in Vorbereitung und Durchführung des Westkriegs*, 1920.
[2] G. Ritter, *Der Schlieffen Plan* (Munich: Oldenbourg Verlag, 1956). English translation *The Schlieffen Plan*, foreword by B. H. Liddell Hart (London: Oscar Wolff, 1958).

ing the German government, he continued, even after retirement, to find a justification for his impossible plan, reportedly expiring with the words, "It must come to a fight. Whatever happens, make the right wing strong."

For years after 1918 the Schlieffen Plan was reckoned one of the most "scientific" military planning exercises ever undertaken. Schlieffen's admirers blamed its failure on Moltke's deviations from it. But really it provides a classic example of the highly professional officer who becomes mesmerized by his own theoretical creation.

Notwithstanding all the care lavished on the plan, its oversights were staggering. The greatest strategic development in Europe since Napoleon's time had been railway building. As Sir Basil Liddell Hart has said, the key to success in a scythelike sweep such as Germany now contemplated was its speed compared with that of the enemy's reaction. But although Schlieffen's war games were repeatedly concerned with the capacity of the German and Belgian railway systems, and actually revealed numerous bottlenecks in them, they quite failed to allow for the capacity of the French. So Moltke was taken by surprise when in 1914 the French responded to the slow-footed German left wheel by switching reinforcements on their rail network centered on Paris. Equally amazing was the failure of the Germans to appreciate the defensive advantage of new weapons such as the machine gun and the quick-firing French "75." Nor does the German General Staff seem to have been aware of the paralyzing effect of barbed wire, although this had been demonstrated in the Russo-Japanese war of 1904.

More important still, the German war gamers failed to take any account of the moral and political factors that were bound to affect their projected campaign. Schlieffen himself seems never to have doubted that "little" Belgium would let the German armies through. If the Belgian government showed signs of resistance, he planned to bring it to heel by a "terror" bombardment of Belgian cities. In 1914 Moltke still believed that the Belgians could be persuaded to "form up along the roads" and salute the invaders as they marched in. Similar indifference was shown towards the British. Half the German Staff thought that they would never intervene. The other half hoped they would attempt a naval landing in Schleswig-Holstein and "be taught a lesson." But when it became clear in 1914 that the British would send troops to Belgium, the Kaiser was thrown into something like panic.

Finally there was Schlieffen's failure to consider the economic consequences of a long war if quick victory proved beyond Germany's grasp. For it seems to have been an unspoken premise of his war games that if, after eight or nine weeks, the German attack ground to a halt, the French would be prepared to sit down and discuss honorable terms for Germany's withdrawal from their territory.

Now, a question may be asked of the Schlieffen Plan which may be asked about other great follies based on war-game "solutions." Did it fail because the games concerned were inherently misleading, or were the answers deliberately "bent" to support preconceived military policies?

We have seen how Schlieffen underrated the resilience of Germany's opponents. One reason for this was undoubtedly his assumption that they would be motivated by the same largely technical considerations that governed German military thinking. Such lack of imagination was common in the German army, and the constant playing of war games in which each side was confronted by a mental replica of itself almost certainly made it worse. In the case of "free" war games the problem was aggravated by uniform solutions imposed by General Staff umpires, trained on the principle that the army should "think with one mind." "Rigid" war games produced their own brand of mental rigidity. For although rules like Naumann's awarded advantages to the buoyant attacker, they neglected to allow any moral counterbalance to troops defending their homeland. So in August–October 1914 the German high command was repeatedly baffled by the behavior of opponents who did not carry Naumann's tables in their pockets to show them when they were beaten.

Whether the outcomes of war games were deliberately bent is an intriguing question. We know that the Kaiser, as Commander-in-chief, liked to turn up at war games in helmet and spurs, and insisted on winning those in which he took part. Schlieffen, of course, was not the Kaiser; but all his memoranda on the projected war against France show a personal weakness. Despite the awkward outcome of quite a number of games, he continued to evade the central fact that the right wing could never be made strong enough for its gigantic task. As Liddell Hart again observes,

> . . . . he seems to have taken the technician's view that his duty was fulfilled if he did the utmost with the means available. . . . He did not consider that he had the higher responsibility of warning the Emperor and the Chancellor that the chances of success were small compared with the risks. And although his operational experience in war games was acclaimed by many of his subordinates, it was never tested in war.[3]

The fact is that German war-game outcomes were readily accepted if they did not upset, or better still if they positively encouraged, the dreams of those who devised them. (One popularly accepted outcome was that garrison forces in an entrenched camp never ventured out until attacked. In 1914 this led to Alexander von Kluck's disastrous decision not to continue with the encirclement of Paris but to fall on the French mobile forces on his left.) But when they conflicted with the grand design, good reasons could always be found for disregarding them. The Schlieffen Plan might well have evolved in the form it did, even if war games had never been invented. But this does not mean that games played an insignificant part. What they did was to give the Schlieffen Plan a wholly specious scientific aura, which in turn served to justify the vast mobilization scheme which could not be halted in the 1914 crisis.

[3] Ritter, *op. cit.*

War games played no comparable part in British military planning at this period, largely for temperamental reasons. There was a tendency to obey tradition and instinct, and, in the Army, an antipathy for "professionalism." There was also a split between those who thought a British expeditionary force could affect a military clash in Europe and those who believed that Britain and the Empire could best be defended by the offensive power of the Royal Navy.

Yet there was a brief exception to this general tendency, when German methods were borrowed to examine the possibility of British land operations in Europe.

For years after the Crimean war of 1854–56 the Government and the War Office had been plagued with fears of an expansionist Russia whose agents they forever saw flitting through the mountain passes into northern India. But after the turn of the century one or two officers at the War Office began to see in Anglo-German trade rivalry, and German aspirations to naval supremacy, a threat from a different direction. In 1902 suspicions of Germany's intentions were expressed by Major General "Wully" Robertson, the rough-cut private who had risen to become head of the Foreign Section of the Military Intelligence Department, and Major General Nicholson, an old friend of Spenser Wilkinson, who had become Director of Military Operations. In 1903 the Secretary of State for War, Hugh Arnold-Forster, another of Wilkinson's friends, gave orders for the circulation among the Committee of Imperial Defence of a memorandum on Germany's growing strength.

One of the first threats considered was that of a German invasion of the British Isles, which had already been discussed quite openly in the German press. But the memorandum did not examine the specific possibility of a war arising from a violation of Belgian neutrality. This was left until 1905 when the newly formed General Staff decided to consider the results of a German invasion in a war game. The game's main purpose was supposed to be instructional, but it became the basis of British military planning for years to come.

The game was umpired by Nicholson's successor as DMO, Major General J. M. Grierson, an authority on the German army.

In a preparatory paper [4] Grierson found that the central plain of Belgium north of the Meuse, with its roads, railways, and open space, was more favorable to a German outflanking march than the hilly plateau of the south. He also found serious deficiencies in the Belgian defenses. Theoretically the Meuse was to be defended by the two great fortresses at Liège and Namur, while Antwerp was to be developed as the ultimate citadel and a landing place for troops from England— thought to be the most reliable guarantor of Belgian neutrality. According to Military Intelligence, nearly half the Belgian army was to garrison the fortresses, the remainder acting as a 100,000-strong field army against the invaders.

The weakness of the Belgian defenses lay partly in the fortress system. The outer forts at Antwerp left a fourteen-mile-wide gap through which the enemy could enter to bombard both the second line and the *enceinte*. (The Meuse fortresses were considered satisfactory, but the game was to show that this was not true of the one at Huy.) The gravest weakness, however, was in the size of the Belgian army which, with a war strength of 170,000, could not provide both fortress garrisons and an adequate field army.

Grierson decided that the Germans were likely to make an outflanking move because of the strength of the French main defenses. But he also thought the move was unsound because of deficiencies in the Belgian railway system. These would oblige the Germans to march largely on foot, with the result that the armies assigned to outflank the French would

[4] Papers relating to the game are to be found in Records of a Strategic War Game, Directorate of Military Operations, War Office. Public Record Office, London. W.O. 33/364 (A 1017).

not make contact with the latter before the twenty-first day. During this time, he thought, the size of the detachment sent through Belgium would gravely weaken the Germans in "decisive" battles at the other end of the front, in Lorraine.

As for British intervention, Grierson doubted the wisdom of it. Circumstances had changed since Napoleon's times, and the Continental mass armies were liable to swamp Britain's limited forces. It would be better to give only token assistance and retain freedom to wage a maritime war against Germany "until she is forced to let go her prize."

Grierson directed that for the purposes of the game it should be assumed that war had broken out between France and Germany on January 1, 1905. At this time neither side had the help of allies. Germany had taken the initiative with an offensive against the French defenses between Sedan and Belfort; but after two months, when these attacks had failed, had decided to outflank the French by passing north through Belgium with six army corps, three cavalry divisions, and two reserve army corps—more than a quarter of a million men. It was assumed that Britain would be brought into war by this violation of Belgian neutrality.

There were three "sides" in the game. The British commander-in-chief was played by Colonel C. E. Callwell, who was to become Deputy Director of Operations in 1914; the German commander-in-chief by Robertson; and the Belgian commander by another staff officer, Major A. Lynden-Bell. Each was assisted by several officers from the Military Operations and Intelligence branches.

In their preliminary "appreciations" the British and Germans agreed that Germany's first object on entering Belgium would be to find and destroy the Belgian field army, or at least to prevent its joining up with the British expeditionary force. This led the Germans to choose the southern route through Belgium rather than the alternative of crossing the Meuse below Liège, passing through Dutch territory and then wheeling south across the Sambre. For although the latter was easier, and offered the advantage of separating the British and Belgians, it would gravely expose German communications.

But between the British and the Belgians there were differences. Callwell, as British commander-in-chief, laid stress on the fact that without the defeat of the Belgian field army and the capture of Antwerp, the German movement would be so delayed, and the numbers needed for its flank protection so increased, that the French would have time to concentrate in the threatened area. He therefore wanted the Belgians to concentrate in the north, protecting Antwerp and effecting an Anglo-Belgian linkup. Against this the "Belgian" commander, while agreeing that the Germans would *like* to separate the British and Belgian forces, expressed doubt that they could move north of the Meuse with only 250,000 men. He also argued that if Belgium appeared to give up her southern road system without a struggle, she could be accused of half-heartedly defending her neutrality, with serious political consequences. In the end he concentrated the field army in the south, relying on the railways to redeploy northwards if necessary.

The need for the British and Belgians to link up was fairly obvious. But what the war game revealed was that current British mobilization and shipping arrangements could not achieve this. For the dispatch of three army corps and three cavalry brigades, which would take seven days to mobilize, the Admiralty envisaged a shuttle service by forty-two vessels. But the Admiralty's ability to fit out shipping was so limited that only twenty-two transports would be available on the tenth day and the full service not before the seventeenth. So the move could not be completed until the thirty-fourth day, and every unit would need twenty-four hours after arrival in which to deploy. (In the game the German players, who had not been told of these limited preparations, assumed that it would take even longer.)

The game was played between January and May, partly with the aid of a German cycling map which gave excellent details of byroads in the south Belgian provinces. The Germans advanced the greater part of their forces south of the Meuse, but passed a cavalry division, and later an infantry division, north of Liège as a feint. This was entirely successful and the Belgians were obliged to withdraw their army to protect Antwerp and the British landings. Later they operated against German communications from the cover of the fortified line of the Meuse. Meanwhile the Germans moved westwards across the Ourthe, ready to operate northwestwards against Huy or to advance on Dinant. Robertson, believing that the British were far away and the French forces growing round Givet on the Franco-Belgian border, now decided to waste no more time with the Belgians and to continue the advance on Dinant immediately. On the thirteenth day of British mobilization an Anglo-Belgian force managed to make a thrust against German communications near Ciney, fifteen miles east of Dinant. At this point Grierson terminated the game, saying that although Ciney might have been taken, the Anglo-Belgian force would eventually have been forced to retire by the superior German forces coming up.

In his adjudication, on May 24th, Grierson sided with the "Belgian" commander in his politico-military argument for concentrating his forces in the south, despite the correctness of the "British" counterargument from a purely military standpoint. But his main point concerned the time needed to put the British expeditionary force into the field. He greatly feared that by the time the British arrived the Belgian army would already have been defeated, and he wondered whether some troops might not have been sent sooner by ordinary mail steamer to lend Belgium moral support. Despite the Anglo-Belgian move towards Ciney on March 13th he concluded that once the Germans had secured their communications, their further advance westwards "could not have been materially interfered with . . . until the arrival of the greater portion of British troops." [5]

The developments envisaged in the war game differed greatly from what actually happened in 1914. Many more German troops were then involved, and the violation of Belgium was not delayed two months while the Germans tried to break into France's eastern defenses. Nevertheless the game correctly drew attention to Anglo-Belgian weaknesses and, as a result, was to have an important impact on British military planning.

Soon after it was held, the question whether Germany would violate Belgian neutrality in a war against France came under discussion at the Foreign Office, and the Permanent Undersecretary was authorized by Balfour, the Prime Minister, to ask the General Staff three questions. What military advantages might Germany, or France, expect to obtain from such a violation? Would the Belgian army be able to offer any effective resistance by holding Namur and Liège? And what time would be required to put two British army corps into Antwerp?

The General Staff answered that Belgium was unlikely to be invaded at the outset because of the formidable political complications, but that one of the belligerents, particularly Germany, might find the invasion of Belgium "imperative" after deadlock developed on the main front. Belgium, it thought, could offer no prolonged resistance, though the hostile advance might be temporarily checked with the help of the field army. The landing of two British army corps would take twenty-three days, assuming that the first twenty transports were ready on the tenth day.

These replies were clearly based on the war game, and the anxieties they reflected were to lead within weeks to the opening of talks with the Chief of the Belgian Staff, General

5 Abt Associates, Inc., "Counter-Insurgency Game Design Feasibility and Evaluation Study," 1965.

Ducarne. The most far-reaching conclusion drawn from the war game, however, was that since a German invasion of Belgium could be expected to succeed, France could not be expected to resist an attack on her own. This resulted, after 1906, in staff talks with the French also, and in the evolution of the Anglo-French Entente, on the strength of which France mobilized in 1914.

While the British were revising the number of horse transports required to take their cavalry from Londonderry to Antwerp, and the Germans were running thousands of imaginary troop trains to deployment areas west of the Rhine, war games were in vogue with the other Great Powers. In France, after an unenthusiastic start, games devised by the École Supérieure de Guerre became general for all staffs and regiments after 1900. In Italy a version of von Trotha's rigid *Kriegsspiel* had been played since 1873. The Austro-Hungarian army, believing that German war games had caused its defeat in 1866, had been trying to catch up ever since, and by 1911 could boast three types of war game for medical officers alone. In Turkey the toy which Moltke had explained to Chosref Pasha was now prescribed by field service regulations. Only Russia flagged.

The Czar had approved instructional war games in 1875, and in 1903 a large-scale game map was issued by the commander-in-chief, General Sheviliev. Each year strategic war games were conducted by senior officers. But Russia faced serious problems. There was a shortage of competent directors, and for want of competence, many of the results obtained through the use of war games failed to match expectations. Finally there existed "a general lack of interest in the game on the part of many of the higher commanders, a tendency to adhere to rigid models, and an appalling lack of basic military knowledge on the part of the participants." [6]

[6] J. P. Young, "A Survey of Historical Developments in War Games" (mimeo). MS P-094, Department of the Army, Washington, D.C. Also as staff paper ORO-SP-98, Operations Research Office, Johns Hopkins University, Bethesda, Maryland, 1959.

Nevertheless, spurred on to improve their military efficiency after their defeat by the Japanese in the war of 1905, the Russians addressed themselves to war games more seriously. In April 1914 the General Staff staged a large-scale war game to work out its strategy for the invasion of East Prussia, which Russia had promised to undertake if the Germans attacked France. In the game the part of the Russian commander-in-chief was played by the sixty-six-year-old War Minister, Vladimir Sukhomlinov. The choice could have been happier, for Sukhomlinov believed he had learned all there was to know about war in a cavalry charge against the Turks in 1877, and would proudly boast that he had not read a military textbook for twenty-five years.

Despite this and other disadvantages, the game of April produced an important lesson. The Russian First Army, which had been allotted the more northerly of the two invasion routes into East Prussia, arrived on the battlefield six days ahead of the Second Army, whose route was more difficult. As a result, the two armies became separated and the game showed that they would thus be soundly defeated. Just how accurately the game exposed this tactical error was to be seen four months later when the two army commanders, Rennenkampf and Samsonov, went into war with the same armies they had commanded in the game.[7]

By an oversight Sukhomlinov had not changed the original timetable. Rennenkampf's First Army never made contact with Samsonov's Second, and both were annihilated in the battle of Tannenberg.

One might have expected the lessons of 1914 to discredit war games in Germany. But they did not. During the war itself, games continued to be used in attempts to devise an escape from the deadlock of trench warfare.

In 1918 the German High Command ordered the rehearsal of its spring offensive in a strategic game played at Crown

[7] N. Golovin, *The Russian Army in the World War* (trans.), New Haven: Yale, 1931.

Prince Rupprecht's Army Corps headquarters. The game showed how small were the prospects of a decisive success. Nevertheless, it was the slim chance of victory, not the odds against it, which characteristically caught the imagination of the High Command and caused it to squander another quarter of a million lives before Germany's defeat.

After 1918 war games received a new impetus because of the restrictions imposed on the size of Germany's armed forces by the Treaty of Versailles. With only 100,000 men there could be no large-scale maneuvers. So the army fell back on what it called "theoretical exercises" to practice officers in the formulation of orders and the making of plans for forces that did not yet exist.

The most interesting war game of the *Reichswehr* period was conducted in 1929 by General Erich von Manstein, then a young staff officer. It was the first on record to pay serious attention to political factors—the prototype, in fact, of politico-military games played by American policy makers today.

Manstein recalls that he was asked to game the possibility —"in those days unfortunately not impossible"—of political tension leading to a Polish attack on East Prussia or Upper Silesia.

> I suggested to the chief of the *Truppenamt* that the war game proper should be preceded by a political game in which the Foreign Ministry participated. He immediately agreed. My suggestion was prompted by the following reasoning: we should not be able to withstand a Polish attack for long on our own. But if Poland's allies were to support her, the position would be hopeless within a few days. It was therefore important . . . to avoid anything which could be regarded by France or Czechoslovakia as a *casus foederis*. Furthermore German policy . . . had to give the League of Nations no chance of avoiding its duty in condemning Polish aggression.[8]

8 F. J. McHugh, "Fundamentals of War Gaming," 3rd edition (mimeo), Newport, R.I., U.S. Naval War College, 1966.

The diplomatic-military game, aimed at finding a balance between the needs of defense and those of diplomacy, was observed by the head of the Foreign Ministry, von Bülow. The head of the political department, Köpke, played the President of the League, and two other senior officials the German and Polish Foreign Ministers. Military roles were taken by Army staff officers.

> We gamed the development of activities by Polish irregulars until the intervention of the Polish army and the formal outbreak of war. . . . At the same time the two Foreign Ministers had to compose Notes to the League Council in the hope of influencing it in their countries' favor. Thus Counsellor von Rintelen, who played the Polish Foreign Minister, had to convince Geneva that only German provocation obliged Poland to act. His German opposite number had to stress the growing threat from Polish actions. Herr von Rintelen proved far superior. His ability to invent German provocations left his adversary speechless.[9]

Köpke, as League President, seems to have given an equally brilliant performance. He was, says Manstein, a master of Geneva phraseology who

> . . . produced soothing answers, offers to send a commission, wrangles about the powers of such a commission—in short, everything we were to see later on in other situations, but no energetic measures which would really have deterred aggression.
>
> The diplomatic-military curtain raiser was very interesting. It showed what kind of lawlessness we should have to reckon with from the Polish troublemakers, and also how carefully we should have to weigh up every defense measure that could be used to whitewash Polish aggression. . . .

Manstein does not elaborate on the reversal of the German and Polish positions in 1939. He merely observes that the Foreign Ministry officials seemed impressed with the game.

[9] *Ibid.*

"We were hoping," he adds, "that they would take a leaf out of our book, so that we could avoid stumbling into a war nobody wanted, as in 1914. We could not foresee that the close association between the Army and the Foreign Ministry would be severed by Hitler, or that foreign policy would one day be in the hands of a man who deliberately steered towards war."

Certainly under Hitler war games were put to more warlike purposes. In the elaborate system developed in the 1930s games would start with a briefing of army commanders by the general commanding the army group. The army commander then instructed divisional commanders, and so on down the line, until even company commanders were familiar with the problem under study. Regimental war games were obligatory one night per week in winter.

But one game stands out in interest. In 1938, when Hitler announced his intention of destroying Czechoslovakia, the army Chief, General Ludwig Beck, raised objections. When Hitler dismissed these, Beck resorted to professional advice. Instead of holding the annual "Chief's tour" he gave selected officers a war-game problem based on the intended attack. The object was not merely to test the feasibility of the operation but to ascertain its likely duration and consequences. Although the problem was presented in more favorable political and military conditions than could reasonably have been expected, the answers produced confirmed Beck's view that however well the campaign against Czechoslovakia might go, it would be a Pyrrhic victory with catastrophic results for Germany and Europe. The Munich agreement prevented the game's prediction from being put to the test. Beck, a brave and upright soldier, resigned his post, and died in 1944 for his part in the July plot.

With the outbreak of World War II, war gaming underwent a change. It was partly due to scientific developments, which we shall describe in Chapter 3, but more generally to the fact that those who conducted games could now draw on current operational experience.

In the winter of 1939–40 the German *Wehrmacht* used its Polish experience as a basis for games to study the problems of deployment and initial operations in the forthcoming campaign in the West. The main problem was to decide where the first thrust should be made, and how to overcome the obstacle of the Ardennes with motorized forces. The games, lasting several days, were held under the Assistant Chief of Staff, General von Stülpnagel. There was also a grand tactical map exercise held at Army headquarters at Zossen and supplemented by trips along the Dutch and Belgian borders.

In the war game the Blue force was commanded by officers of the Army Supreme Command (OKH) and Red by the head of the "Foreign Armies, West" branch of Military Intelligence. The game was based on German operational plans and the enemy situation as it was known at the time. The Red commander was not supposed to act according to German principles but to adopt decisions which the enemy command was thought likely to make. In the words of a German officer, the purpose was "to provide a chance of raising and discussing several controversial problems within a specially selected and critical circle. Therefore the exercise did not proceed in the form of a continuing game, but rather by leaps and bounds. . . ." [10]

The map exercise was used to check whether the time allowed for crossing the Ardennes was likely to prove correct. Aerial photographs as well as maps were used, and field units had to report the exact strengths and march intervals of all the units involved down to individual repair trucks. The capacities of roads, secondary routes, and parking places were entered on large-scale maps so as to give an exact picture of where every column and individual vehicle was located

[10] Quoted in Department of the Army, Office of the Chief of Military History, "War Games," MS P-094, Washington, D.C., 1952.

at any given moment. Every six hours a test was made to ascertain when, where, and how interruptions might arise due to enemy action, traffic congestion, refueling, and the state of the roads.

Actual events in May 1940 showed that the troops covered their march distances more quickly than in the war game, probably because the French and Belgian air forces did not intervene as effectively as had been feared. But both the game and the map exercise gave the Chief of Staff, Halder, useful information when making his final operational plan and, according to German officers, contributed greatly to the smoothness of the initial phase of the attack.

After the occupation of France a war game was held at Turcoing to examine aspects of Operation Sealion, the proposed invasion of the British Isles. The technical difficulties it revealed contributed to the project's abandonment. Another game "Otto" was conducted to prepare for Operation Barbarossa, the invasion of Russia. But perhaps the most remarkable game on the German side was one held by OKH on the eve of the American offensive in the Ardennes in 1944. The staff of Model's Fifth Army had just begun a game to rehearse defense measures against an American attack between the Fifth and Seventh Armies, when news arrived that the attack had already started. The story goes that Model calmly ordered the game to continue, using reports from the front as his game material and transforming game orders into actual operation orders to his troops.[11]

Though similar games were used by the Anglo-American staffs in planning the great landings in North Africa and Normandy, and an impromptu war game appears to have been played by the British and American missions in Moscow in 1945 to decide whether the Russians could fulfill their promise to attack Japan within thirty days of victory in Europe,[12] war games played a smaller part in Allied war plan-

11 Young, *op. cit.*
12 Information to the author by one of the participants.

ning than was the case with the Axis Powers. The British Air Staff is said to have conducted a number of exercises which "proved" its ability to win a war with Germany by strategic bombing, and the Army to have conducted games which established the impregnability of Singapore. But if so, the evidence has been tactfully expunged from the records. Nor is it easy to find confirmation of the intriguing story that the French High Command refused to sanction a war game that sought to examine the impregnability of the Maginot Line.

The chief user of war games on the Allied side was the United States Navy, which in 1922 had modernized its tactical games with a fire effect system based on actual armaments and ships. Strategic games, played across a network of pneumatic tubes for message carrying, were used to explore almost every situation that could arise in a war in the Pacific. Consequently, five years after the war ended, Admiral Nimitz, the architect of American naval victory, could tell students at the Naval War College: "The war with Japan has been [enacted] in the game room here by so many people and in so many different ways that nothing that happened during the war was a surprise—absolutely nothing except the Kamikaze tactics towards the end of the war; we had not visualized those." [13] The palm was fairly awarded, though Nimitz omitted to mention Pearl Harbor.

That high-level war games were played by the Soviet army cannot be doubted. We have seen that they were used in the Czarist army, and the technique was probably carried into the Red army by Tukhachevsky. About 1939 the Soviet High Command is believed to have conducted a game with far-reaching consequences. Played before the signing of the Molotov–Ribbentrop Pact, it examined the possible course of a war with Nazi Germany and produced the answer that such a war would go very badly indeed for Russia. Up to this time Stalin had based his defense plans on a proposal to

[13] McHugh, *op. cit.*

launch a strategic counteroffensive. Allegedly as a result of the game, Soviet strategy was revised. It now became Stalin's policy to prepare for an initial withdrawal and reserve the offensive for later in the war. But when Hitler attacked in 1941, the Soviet war machine was only half readjusted, and it became necessary to yield much more ground than intended.

The most chastening experience with war games in World War II fell to the Japanese. The German *Kriegsspiel* had been adopted in Japan at the end of the nineteenth century and may have played some part in the training of the Japanese forces which defeated the Russians in 1905. Thirty-five years later the Japanese surpassed their mentors by setting up the Total War Research Institute in Tokyo. At the Institute officers of all three services and officials of the Foreign Ministry and other departments conducted war games to determine Japanese policy. The games resulted in detailed military and economic plans which were put into effect on December 8, 1941—though at the time the games were played, Pearl Harbor itself had not been specifically planned. Far from being simple two-sided "Blue versus Red" exercises the Japanese games involved numerous teams to represent political forces in the Axis, the Soviet Union, the United States, Britain, Thailand, the Netherlands, China, Korea, the Dutch East Indies, Manchuria, and French Indo-China. As such, the players represented different national aims and conflicting interests, though coalitions could exist among both friendly and enemy elements.[14]

In August 1941 further war games of a purely military character were conducted at the War College in Tokyo. These were largely concerned with naval operations and examined the advantages of an attack on Pearl Harbor. Among the needs revealed was that of a successful method of torpedo

[14] Young, *op. cit.*

attack against ships in confined shallow waters. There followed a strenuous effort by the Japanese to alter their torpedoes to secure quick-leveling after entry into the water. One month before the attack they succeeded in fitting wooden stabilizers to the rear fins, which produced satisfactory leveling in the forty-five-foot depth of water available.[15]

Other games at the Institute and War College resulted in a carefully prepared timetable for occupying Malaya, Burma, the Dutch East Indies, and the Central Pacific islands. In February 1942 a game was held aboard the battleship *Yamato*, flagship of the Combined Fleet, to test tentative plans for the destruction of the British Far East Fleet, the capture of Ceylon, and ultimately a junction with German forces whose advance was expected into Egypt and the Near East.

What might have happened had this junction been made is one of the great "ifs" of history. On the German side it was prevented by Hitler's commitment in Russia, and on the Japanese side by the refusal of the army to transfer the necessary troops from the Russo-Japanese border. Balked in their westward ambition, Japanese naval planners returned their attention to the Pacific; and in planning the second phase of their Pacific offensive, enacted the most fateful war game of the whole war.

Early in May, Admiral Yamamoto, the Commander-in-chief of the Japanese Combined Fleet, summoned his officers to another series of games aboard the *Yamato*. For most of them it was the first intimation of the roles they were to play in a major operation.

The starting point of the game series was the invasion of Midway Island, almost equidistant from Japan and the United States. But on this first move hung a grandiose program: the capture of the Aleutians, of New Caledonia and the Fiji Islands, air strikes against Sydney, and finally a full-scale assault of Hawaii. According to an eye-witness "the eyes of

[15] E. Girard, in "Proceedings of Second War Gaming Symposium (mimeo), Washington Operations Research Council, 1964.

many sparkled" as the scheme was unfolded. But among those in the know, several commanders already had grave doubts about the Midway operation, which would have to be carried out without shore-based air support. The enemy, in contrast, would have both shore-based air strength and still undamaged carrier forces, thanks to the escape of his carriers at Pearl Harbor four months before. These points were made forcefully to Yamamoto, but he brushed them aside. The story of the game is taken up by a Japanese naval officer:

Except for the staff of Combined Fleet Headquarters, all those taking part were amazed at this formidable program, which seemed to have been dreamed up with a great deal more imagination than regard for reality. Still more amazing, however, was the manner in which every operation from the invasion of Midway and the Aleutians down to the assault on Johnston and Hawaii was carried out in the games without the slightest difficulty. This was due in no small measure to the high-handed conduct of Rear Admiral Ugaki, the presiding officer, who frequently intervened to set aside rulings made by the umpires.

In the tabletop maneuvers, for example, a situation developed in which the Nagumo [main carrier] Force underwent a bombing attack by enemy land-based aircraft while its own planes were off attacking Midway. In accordance with the rules, Lieutenant Commander Okumiya, Carrier Division Four staff officer, who was acting as an umpire, cast dice to determine the bombing results and ruled that there had been nine enemy hits on the Japanese carriers. Both *Akagi* and *Kaga* were listed as sunk. Admiral Ugaki, however, arbitrarily reduced the number of enemy hits to only three, which resulted in *Kaga*'s still being ruled sunk but *Akagi* only slightly damaged. To Okumiya's surprise, even this revised ruling was subsequently canceled and *Kaga* reappeared as a participant in the next part of the games covering the New Caledonia and Fiji Islands invasions. The verdicts of the umpires regarding the results of air fighting were similarly juggled, always in favor of the Japanese forces.

The value of the games was also impaired by the fact that the participating staff officers from several major operational commands, including the Nagumo Force and the shore-based Eleventh Air Fleet, had had little time to study the operations to be tested. The result was that they could only play out their parts like puppets, with the staff of Combined Fleet Headquarters pulling the strings. There, the somewhat reckless manner in which the Nagumo Force operated evoked criticism, and the question was raised as to what plan the Force had in mind to meet the contingency that an enemy carrier task force might appear on its flank while it was executing its scheduled air attack on Midway. The reply given by the Nagumo Force staff officer present was so vague as to suggest that there was no such plan. . . . Indeed, in the actual battle this is precisely what happened.

Following the conclusion of the war games on May 4, two additional days were devoted to study and briefing conferences concerning the Midway operations. Various recommendations were advanced for making changes in the operational plan, but for the most part they got nowhere. In particular, almost all the participating fleet commanders . . . strongly urged postponement of the invasion date in order to allow more time for battle preparations. Rear Admiral Ugaki, however, asserted that this was impossible because a postponement, unless it were for an entire month, would mean that there would be inadequate moonlight for night maneuvering off the invasion beaches.[16]

What happened at the battle of Midway four weeks later was that the Americans, having intercepted Japanese radio messages and recalled their carriers from various parts of the Pacific, assembled to meet the attack. The Japanese approached in three groups: to the north, Vice-Admiral Nagumo's carriers; to the west an invasion fleet of transports; to the northwest, widely separated from the carrier force, Yamamoto's main battle fleet.

[16] M. Fuchida and M. Okumiya, *Midway, the Battle that Doomed Japan* (Annapolis, Md.: United States Naval Institute, 1955; London: Hutchinson, 1957).

Thanks to fog, the Japanese carrier force eluded detection until it had launched its first air strike against Midway. But as soon as Midway reported the attack, the American carriers closed in. After ineffective attacks by torpedo bombers and shore-based aircraft, fifty-four dive bombers of the United States carriers *Yorktown* and *Enterprise* fell on the Japanese carriers while their bombers were being rearmed. *Kaga* was hit by four bombs, *Soryu* by three, and *Akagi* by two. Fires were started, ammunition exploded, and all three ships went down. *Hiryu,* though her aircraft dispatched the United States carrier *Yorktown,* was also sunk. The battle cost the Japanese two-thirds of their big carriers; it also cost them the war.

3

THE END OF AMATEURISM

IF WAR GAMES were less spectacularly used on the Allied side in World War II, the reason is that more reliable methods were adopted for the appraisal of Allied strategy. Obviously this did not prevent major errors, but the errors can more often be traced to a failure to use the new methods than to a failure of the methods themselves.

The innovation began in 1939 with the work of a small group of civilian scientists assigned to RAF Fighter Command headquarters at Stanmore, on the northern outskirts of London. Their task was to help the Air Force with early problems in the operation of radar, the "secret weapon" whose development had begun only four years before the war. When their work on radar was finished, some of the group were asked to remain with the Command to investigate more general operational problems, such as statistical problems involving the wastage rates of pilots and aircraft.

From this unplanned beginning there grew up an activity called Operational Research which, in the military context, has been described as the application of quantitative reasoning to problems of weapons, tactics, and strategy. It merits a historical digression because ultimately it gave rise to a whole complex of military analytical techniques of which present-day war games are only one.

Quantitative reasoning had first been applied to military problems in 1914–15 when the British aeronautical pioneer F. W. Lanchester (1868–1946) published a series of papers on the relationship between victory, numerical superiority, and firepower superiority in battle. The papers were collected in his book *Aircraft in Warfare,* published in 1916.

One of Lanchester's conclusions is known as the N^2 Law which, on the assumption that all units of two opposing forces can engage in combat simultaneously, shows (a) that numerical superiority may be relatively more important than superiority in weapon performance; and (b) that to achieve victory it is necessary to employ all one's available fighting units in a single force and to split up the enemy. There was nothing new about the latter principle, which had been adopted by countless great captains in history, including Nelson at Trafalgar. What was new was the mathematical demonstration of it. Lanchester made an analysis of Nelson's tactics, showing that they were the best he could have adopted in the light of the N^2 Law.[1]

---

1 A simplified treatment of Lanchester's Theorem is given by Prof. P. M. S. Blackett (*Studies of War* [Edinburgh: Oliver and Boyd, 1962]). Suppose A units of one force of hitting power α are engaged with B units of hitting power β. Suppose further that the engagement is of such a kind that the firepower of force A is directed equally against all units of B and vice versa; then the rate of loss of the two forces is given by

$$\frac{dA}{dt} = -k\,\beta\,B \text{ and } \frac{dA}{dt} = k\,\alpha\,A$$

where k is constant.

The strength of the two factors is defined as equal when their fractional losses are equal, i.e., when

Although Lanchester's a priori approach to operational problems continues to hold great theoretical interest, its practical uses proved to be small; and when the Stanmore scientists, and subsequently other operational research groups, were called in to help improve the efficiency of the British war effort twenty-five years later, the urgency of the times obliged them to adopt empirical and more practical methods.

One of the first major successes of the new methods occurred in 1941 at the operational research section in RAF Coastal Command under Professor P. M. S. Blackett. It followed the arrival of a scientist, Evan Williams, who was working on the possibility of a proximity fuse for depth charges dropped by antisubmarine aircraft.

Before going ahead with his proximity fuse, Williams decided to analyze reports of air attacks on U-boats. For such attacks it was necessary for the patrolling aircraft to sight the U-boat as it cruised on the surface, for speed or to recharge its batteries. But as soon as the U-boat sighted the aircraft, the U-boat dived to elude it. Thus the earlier the aircraft was sighted, the deeper would be the U-boat when the attack came. On the assumption that a U-boat would generally sight the patrolling aircraft about two minutes before the latter could attack, Coastal Command had given orders that all depth charges should be set to explode at a depth of 100 feet.

But Williams saw a fallacy in this argument. It might be true that *on the average* a U-boat would sight the aircraft at this distance. But with two minutes' warning the U-boat had so long to dive and move away from the place where it was sighted that the accuracy of the attack was bound to be low. Williams drew attention to the rarer but important occasions

$$\frac{1}{A}\frac{dA}{dt} = \frac{1}{B}\frac{dB}{dt}$$

Using the above relation we get

$$\alpha \, A^2 = B^2$$

Thus the *strength* of a force, on these assumptions, is proportional to the firepower of a unit multiplied by the *square* of the number of units.

when the U-boat failed to sight the aircraft in time and was attacked on or near the surface. In such cases the attack was much more accurate. But because the depth charge was set to explode at 100 feet, the U-boat escaped serious damage. Williams calculated that if the depth setting were reduced to twenty-five feet, the number of successful attacks would be increased two and a half times. When, as a result of his recommendations, this was done, the results were so spectacular that U-boat crews thought the British were using a new and more powerful explosive.[2]

Not long after this, operational research was applied to the problem of reducing heavy convoy losses from attacks by U-boat wolf packs. In 1942 the average convoy consisted of about forty merchantmen protected by six escort vessels, and it was estimated that without air cover about double the number of escorts was needed to give adequate protection. But since aircraft were in short supply, and further escorts were not available, the operational analysts had to look for some other means of cutting down losses. This led them to consider whether they should change the *size* of convoys.

When they investigated the pattern of losses in convoys of various sizes, they found that the percentage losses in large convoys were much lower than those in small ones. Thus convoys of less than forty-five ships were losing an average of 2.6 percent of their vessels in each crossing of the Atlantic, while larger convoys were losing only 1.7 percent. In fact, the same number of ships was lost per convoy whether the convoy was small or large, although the number of escorts provided for small and large convoys was the same.

When this phenomenon was investigated scientifically, the explanation proved absurdly simple, though up to then nobody had thought of it. For, as every schoolboy knows, the area of a circle increases by the square of its radius, whereas the perimeter is directly proportional to the radius. Thus the

2 P. M. S. Blackett, *Studies of War* (Edinburgh: Oliver and Boyd, 1962).

perimeter of a large convoy (whose area was determined by the minimum safe distance between ships) was only slightly larger than that of a small one, and the number of escorts needed to watch it was almost the same. To be precise, it was found that seven escorts could protect a convoy of eighty ships as effectively as six escorts could protect one of forty. At the same time a moment's reflection showed that if a submarine penetrated the escort screen, it was unlikely to sink any more ships in a large convoy than in a small one because of its fixed number of torpedoes.

On receiving this analysis, the Admiralty decided to increase the size of convoys and reduce their number by a third, reallocating a proportion of escort vessels to mobile support groups which went to the aid of convoys under attack. The result was a marked reduction in shipping losses without any extra cost in protective resources.[3]

But the most spectacular application of operational research occurred in the study of explosives. At the start of the war it was believed that a man could be killed by a blast pressure of 5 pounds per square inch. On this calculation the RAF had reckoned to carry out the strategic bombardment of Germany with a small "general purpose" bomb of 250 pounds, much of whose weight lay in a thick iron casing. Incredible as it may seem, the military authorities had conducted no recent experiments to ascertain the scientific facts, which remained undiscovered until a non-Service body, the Civil Defence Research Committee, called in the anatomist and authority on monkeys, Professor Solly Zuckerman.

Zuckerman conducted a series of experiments with goats in trenches and found, by anatomical analogy, that a man had a 50-percent chance of survival after being struck by a blast pressure of 500 pounds per square inch. In other words, blast proved to be 100 times less dangerous than had been sup-

---

[3] Congressional Record. Testimony May 11, 1966, hearings, "Department of Defense Appropriations for 1967," Subcommittee on Department of Defense, House Committee on Appropriations, 89th Congress, 2d Session, part 6.

posed. Later on, using medical evidence from actual bombing, Zuckerman went on to develop the concept of a standardized casualty rate to forecast the average number of casualties resulting from the dropping of a given weight of bombs on areas of varying population intensity. Similarly two other British scientists, Professor J. D. Bernal and Dr. F. Garwood, used new data on bomb effectiveness to forecast the result of a 500-bomber raid on a typical British city—for which they happened to choose Coventry. When Coventry came to be raided by 500 German aircraft on April 11th, 1941, their forecast, based on statistical experiments, was almost exactly confirmed.[4]

It may be seen from these examples that one kind of operational research consists of analyzing how certain weapons perform, or how certain tactics are conducted, in order to improve or counter them. Thousands of such studies were made in World War II. Partly they were based on battle reports; partly on realistic training exercises; partly on laboratory tests in which, for example, a static aircraft would be exposed to antiaircraft shell explosions to ascertain the average distribution of damage to vital components. But there also grew up a "higher" kind of operational research whose object was to suggest more efficient *strategies*. This meant comparing the results of various types of major operation and the cost, in war resources, of achieving them.

For example, an analysis of shipping losses in 1942 showed that air cover for eight hours a day reduced convoy casualties by 64 percent, and that every three sorties by an aircraft saved one merchant ship. As each long-range aircraft made an average of forty sorties before itself being lost, it was able, on the average, to save thirteen ships. The reason for this was that U-boats had to move on the surface in order to keep up with a convoy, but when sighted by aircraft they had to submerge and so lost touch. To overcome this difficulty the

4 Blackett, *op. cit.*

enemy resorted to attacking convoys farther and farther from land, which increased the time the aircraft had to spend flying to and from the convoy and reduced the time available for the task of protecting it. Operational research was directed to discovering the point at which the aircraft would be better employed elsewhere; and the concept used to determine this point was known as the "exchange rate."

The exchange rate in any type of operation is simply the ratio between the efforts put into it and the results got out of it, measured in suitable units. In the air campaign against U-boats the exchange rate which mattered was

$$\frac{\text{FLYING HOURS}}{\text{U-BOAT SIGHTINGS.}}$$

In active U-boat areas this sometimes worked out at less than 100 flying hours to every sighting. But when long approach flights were involved, the number of flying hours often ran into thousands. Calculations suggested that aircraft should be diverted from the mid-Atlantic to attacks on U-boats as they passed between their hunting grounds and their bases in the Bay of Biscay—a transfer of resources which was duly made, with vital consequences in winning the Battle of the Atlantic.

In analyzing the effect of RAF bombing against Germany a more complex exchange rate was used. This involved measuring the cost of delivering a given bomb load in terms of the man-years needed to build and operate the aircraft, compared with the cost to the enemy in terms of providing defenses and making indispensable repairs. The resulting equation

$$\frac{\text{MAN-YEARS IN BOMBING EFFORT/BOMB-TONS DROPPED}}{\text{ENEMY MAN-YEARS ON DEFENSES AND REPAIRS/BOMB-TONS DROPPED}}$$

not only gave a manpower exchange rate but also, when broken down for particular types of aircraft, showed the unexpected effectiveness of Mosquito raids and the superiority of the Lancaster over the Halifax bomber.[5]

When operational research moved on from the analysis of operations which had already taken place to predicting the effectiveness of plans which had yet to be executed, it made use of another mathematically expressed concept, the "constant effectiveness ratio." This showed the *long-term* level of results to be expected from a given type of weapon or activity, which in World War II showed a remarkable consistency in a wide variety of circumstances. For example, the figure of sixty mines laid per ship sunk was found to occur in every aircraft mining campaign in the war—German mines in British ports, British mines in German sea routes, American mines on Japanese sea routes. Similarly the probability that an aircraft would attack a sighted enemy submarine was the same for different types of aircraft in different theaters of war. In submarine operations the effectiveness ratio

$$\frac{\text{JAPANESE SHIPS SUNK}}{\text{TORPEDOES FIRED}}$$

was the same in Japanese coastal waters as in the South China Sea.[6]

The constancy of these ratios, despite a large number of chance events and differences in the ability of individuals involved in operations, had two explanations. First, the differences tended to average out for a series of operations. Secondly, weapons—and even tactics—did not change quickly because of the long time needed to develop new equipment and train men to use it. This meant that so long as operations had been in progress for some time, and tactics had become sufficiently stabilized, data obtained on them could be transferred from the analysis of one operation to that of another with reasonable confidence of producing the right result.

[5] M. Csizmas, "Military Cybernetics in Eastern Europe," *Military Review*, September 1967.
[6] C. Kittel, "The Nature and Development of Operations Research," *Science*, 105:150–53, February 7, 1947.

After the spring of 1943, when Allied forces began to move into Axis territory, it became possible for the first time to analyze operations in relation to their specific purpose. The first opportunity came in North Africa where studies were made of damage inflicted on Tripoli and other Allied air targets. As Professor Zuckerman later put it

> . . . essentially, what was being done was to treat each operation as one might an experiment of a very crude kind. How closely did what was achieved correspond to what we had set out to do? Why were intention and effect not always the same? [7]

The bombing of Tripoli had not actually been *planned* as an experiment. But the experimental approach was more directly followed in planning, executing, and later analyzing, operations leading up to the capture of the island of Pantelleria. The lessons thus learned were subsequently applied to the 1944 pre-D-Day air offensive against the coastal defenses of northern France. Similarly, lessons learned from a detailed analysis of the effects of air attacks on the railway system of Sicily and southern Italy provided the basis of the 1944 plan to destroy the communications network of northwest Europe. Later, when the liberation of northwest Europe made it possible to analyze the effects of this attack also, the projections made on the basis of Mediterranean experience were felt to have been validated.

However, according to Zuckerman,

> . . . there was little opportunity for this kind of analysis of field warfare—largely, I think, because it moved too fast for the results, when they became available, to be applied; also, the situations in field warfare were infinitely more varied than in either sea or air war.

From all this it can be seen that there was nothing theoretical about operational analysis in World War II. (In fact, busi-

[7] S. Zuckerman, "Judgment and Control in Modern Warfare," *Foreign Affairs*, 40:196–212 (January 1962).

ness had used it as a practical technique to study industrial and commercial operations in peacetime.) The scientists saw it simply as the application of scientific discipline to the study of matters which had too long been left to amateurs. They were trained, they felt, "to get down to the fundamentals of a question—to seek out broad underlying principles through a mass of sometimes conflicting and irrelevant data. They know how to handle data and how to guard against the fallacious interpretation of statistics, with the results that they were often able to discredit what the military regarded as 'commonsense' solutions." [8] This was true. But it was also remarkable that the leading operational research groups included not only physicists and mathematicians, but also numerous biologists, zoologists (like Zuckerman), economists, and other "non-exact" scientists. Why was this? The answer, given by the scientists, was that war was too complex, too beset with "unknowns," to lend itself to purely mathematical analysis. Like biology and economics, it contained

> . . . areas where a limited amount of numerical data are available, and such data can be extremely useful in research. Biologists are accustomed to study living organisms, which means dealing with many factors simultaneously when very little may be known about individual factors. To do this they have evolved a special kind of statistics, enabling them to make generalizations in a field where generalizations are often theoretically impossible to establish.[9]

By the time the war ended there was scarcely a field of military activity, on the Allied side, that had not been profoundly affected by operational research. Its impact ranged from improvements in tank gunnery and field engineering to the complete recasting of air and naval procurement programs. If its findings were sometimes overoptimistic (as in the case of the damage inflicted by strategic bombing on German

8 Kittel, *op. cit.*
9 *Ibid.*

war production), at least they were much nearer the mark than the intuitive estimates of military commanders, and they demonstrably saved many lives, and vast resources, that would otherwise have been wasted on unprofitable activities. This made it inevitable that operational research methods developed in the war should be retained as an aid to military planning in the uneasy peace.

At first this presented no difficulty, at least so far as "conventional" forces were concerned. For wartime operations continued to provide a wealth of recent experience on which to work. In addition, investigators could enter ex-enemy territory to discover what had gone on "on the other side of the hill." But as the years passed, and new weapons came into service, wartime experience declined in value; and although new material was provided by the war in Korea, its specialized nature often made it unreliable as a basis for estimating the performance of Allied forces and equipment elsewhere, for example in a possible war against Russia in Europe.

The biggest problems, however, were in the nuclear field. Superficially it might seem that in the first years of peace, operational research, at least in the West, was well placed in this respect. For the ruins of Hiroshima and Nagasaki provided a terrible laboratory in which it was possible to measure the effects of the most powerful weapon then in existence. The atomic bomb had been exploded, not in a test, but in an actual operation. Its blast and incendiary effects could be examined from every angle; its long-term radiation effects could be followed up in the hospitals; and its enormous psychological effect had been demonstrated by the fact that Japan had surrendered.

In fact, this material was of more limited value. Only two bombs had been dropped, equal in destructive power to about 1/300th of all the bombs dropped on Germany during the war. They had been dropped without the enemy suspecting their existence, so that arguably more people might have been exposed to them than would be the case in a true "nuclear war"; and it was not so easy, on reflection, to distinguish their psychological impact from the cumulative effect of previous bombing and the threatened invasion of the Japanese homeland. In retrospect, therefore, it seems likely that contemporary analysis overrated the enduring operational value of the simple A-bomb.

But reflections on this score became purely academic as a result of America's explosion of the hydrogen bomb in 1951, and Russia's explosion of it a year later.

In 1952 an American thermonuclear (hydrogen) device caused the complete disappearance of the island of Elugelab, on which it had been placed, leaving an underwater crater one mile across and 175 feet deep. It released energy equivalent to 5,000,000 tons of TNT, compared with the Hiroshima bomb's equivalent of 20,000 tons, and produced a fireball three and a half miles across, compared with Hiroshima's one-sixth of a mile. But the difference between the H-bomb and the A-bomb was not just one of size. Because of its destructive power the H-bomb made nonsense of all earlier attempts to formulate nuclear war strategies, while posing the problem that henceforth the most critical and costly planning decisions would have to be taken about a weapon whose total effects might never be known until it was too late to do anything about them.

What could operational research do in such a situation? Since actual operational experience was lacking, two other methods of operational study had to be used. From further "laboratory tests" in the Pacific it was possible to make theoretical estimates of the damage produced by various designs of warhead exploded at various altitudes; and from rigorous training exercises it was possible to make estimates of the proportion of bombers that might penetrate one's own or the enemy's defenses. But these could provide no reliable information about the *total* effects of a thermonuclear attack.

Where lack of operational experience mattered even more was with tactical nuclear weapons—atomic artillery and short-range "battlefield" missiles—which came into service in the mid-1950s. Of the H-bomb it could be narrowly argued that it was unnecessary to know its full capabilities with exactitude because the prospect of a retaliation in kind would deter an enemy from using it in the first place. But with tactical nuclear weapons—which some experts imagined could be used as "super-artillery" to make good a shortage of ground troops—it was necessary to know in some detail their likely effect on each side's *control* of the battle as well as the number of civilian casualties that might arise.

How could such questions be answered, let alone titanic strategic questions such as "What size of force is needed to threaten an aggressor with unacceptable damage?" "What life would survive after a major nuclear attack?" or, assuming deterrence should fail, "How many bombers or missiles are needed to *win* a nuclear war?"

At this point our excursion into the history of operational research brings us back to our central theme; for one of the means chosen to offset the lack of operational experience was war games.[10]

As we have seen, the nineteenth-century *Kriegsspiel,* modernized and improved, had been used for the testing of operational plans, particularly on the Axis side, in 1939–45. In the United States its use for training purposes continued at the Army and Navy War Colleges. But the uncertainties caused by the Bomb and the Cold War gave rise to entirely new types of games. In the new environment games were demanded not only for instructing commanders and testing plans, but also for generating ideas, acquiring data, gaining insights into the future, and assisting all kinds of research. Nor was the military machine the only user. Any Department concerned with national security had a potential inter-

---

[10] I have avoided the artificial distinction sometimes made between "war games" and "simulations," where the latter means one-sided computer games. The term "simulation" is reserved for games in social science research, described in Chapter 11.

est in war games, whether as a means of preparing for war or as a way of solving crises. Academic institutions were also deeply involved, because they alone had the skills required to invent the more sophisticated kind of game. Finally, the business world, which had already been ahead of the military in introducing operational research, had an interest in games for the study of economic competition; and some games were of use to both.

In the military sphere, the different types of game resulting from the Cold War could be grouped under four headings:

(1) *"Umpired" games* were a development of the old-style "free" war game, extended in scope. There were no rules, and the general development of the game was left to a "director." Umpired games, like those under some other headings, could be "open" or "closed." "Open" meant that the whole game took place in a single room, so that each side heard the arguments leading to the other's move. "Closed" meant that the teams decided their moves in private. The most important type of umpired game produced by the Cold War was the politico-military game, which we shall see in the next chapter.

(2) *Rigid manual games* were a renaissance of the original *Kriegsspiel*, in which all moves were governed by detailed rules. They were most frequently used to evolve and assess new field tactics. The game was generally played with symbols on a terrain model, which would have been familiar to Reisswitz. But they could also take the form of "bookkeeping" games in which forces were represented by entries on tally sheets. The advantage of rigidity was that alternative tactics could be tested and compared in a series of games all offering similar conditions.

(3) *Machine games,* using electronic computers, were widely adopted to represent a strategic nuclear exchange. They could also be used to represent any kind of warfare involving a high proportion of quantifiable factors, such as

air or sea war. Their appeal, as we shall see, lay in the ability of the computer to handle a vast mass of data quickly. A variation of the machine method was the inclusion of one or more human participants in the game. In this type of game, called a Man-Machine game, the human player might select, say, the size and composition of an attacking force, and the machine would compute the outcome of its engagement with the enemy.

(4) *Mathematical games* included games that could be analyzed by so-called Game Theory (see Chapter 10). They were not war games as most people would recognize them, but highly simplified representations of conflict in which each side generally had two courses of action. Game theory stated the optimum course to take irrespective of which course the other side adopted.

These four categories continue to form the basis of current American war gaming, an activity so vast and diverse as to defy adequate description in a single book. In 1963 there were some 200 officially listed war-game models,[11] excluding many used purely for military training at lower levels. Many were used at more than one establishment and were available for the study of any number of types of armed conflict. Since then the number has probably doubled every two years, and the number of institutions now involved in designing or using games for military research purposes probably exceeds one hundred. How does all this activity combine with other forms of operational analysis?

To answer this question it is necessary to recall that, to meet new demands, the whole process of defense research has undergone great changes since 1945. Many changes would have occurred quite independently of the great uncertainty caused by the development of the Bomb. Apart from the greatly increased cost of modern weapons, the biggest con-

---

[11] Models here mean sets of game rules.

cerns the time taken between first conceiving the requirement for a weapon and actually bringing it into service. In
the 1940s it took only four or five years to develop a major
military aircraft from scratch. Today it may take eight. The
time taken between starting to develop a weapon and its final
withdrawal from service may well be between fifteen and
twenty years. Moreover, it is no longer possible to talk intelligently of "weapons," but only of "weapons systems," because
the aircraft, missile, or space satellite is militarily meaningless
without its associated system of guidance and control radars,
warheads, electronic countermeasures, and so on, the failure
of any of which means the failure of the whole. By the time
such a system enters service it may have to function in a radi-
cally changed technological environment in the shape of, say,
the defenses it will have to penetrate—to say nothing of
changes in the *overall* environment such as the possible disappearance of the enemy or targets against which it was
intended, and their replacement by others.

All this calls for a kind of analysis very different from that
used in 1939–45 when the enemy, the theater, the targets,
and the technological prospects were all more or less known.

The best-known method of forward-looking analysis developed since World War II is called "systems analysis" (a name
also used for its counterpart in industry). Systems analysis has
been described as analysis from an economic viewpoint in
which the word "economic" has a special meaning: not that
of the budgeteer or comptroller who wants to reduce expendi-
tures all round—though it is often accused of serving this end
—but that of the planner seeking the best allocation of limited resources among a variety of competing military demands.

The starting point of any systems analysis is the concept
of a particular system and a variety of alternative systems, and
the environment in which they will operate. This is where
war games come into their own, either by suggesting what the
future environment may be like (generation of scenarios, see

Chapter 9), or by representing the system in such a way that its weaknesses can be highlighted, modifications explored, and alternatives compared. The number of defense projects regularly canceled after great expense suggests that systems analysis does not always prevent the mistakes it is supposed to—though since its rigorous application in both America and Britain cancellations have tended to occur at an earlier stage.

Another new method of operational analysis is based on the mathematical type of game. This esoteric method is intended as a guide to decision making. But although some areas with which it deals, for example a choice of targets in air attack, may be open to abstract treatment, most people would probably agree with Zuckerman that others contain

> . . . parameters of so qualitative a nature that no one could attribute numerical values to them. . . . For example they include such matters as the enemy's intentions as well as his strength and capacity; the resolution of our people; the capacity of a country to restore itself economically when it has suffered a degree of devastation well beyond anything that lies within human comprehension—let alone experience. . . .[12]

In addition to the forms of research just mentioned, war games are also used in the analysis of current operational plans and postures, providing, through "synthetic war," experience not available in the field. To many people, in fact, this may seem their most critical use, since the inevitable artificiality of all games may lead to illusions about one's ability to "prevail" with the plan or posture in real life.

We have spoken of operational research, and war games, in a purely Western context. But this is due to the open-ness of Western sources. It would have been very difficult for the Soviet Union to plan its postwar space and military programs without resort to some form of analysis for deciding military priorities.

[12] Zuckerman, *op. cit.*

The kind of operational research associated with war games is generally treated in the Soviet Union under the heading of cybernetics. Until the mid-1950s this was officially dismissed as a theory of "philosophical obscurantism." But with the increasing use of computers for scientific research, Soviet and East European journals began, between 1959 and 1962, to publish an increasing number of articles on cybernetics. At the 22nd Party Congress in 1961 cybernetics was finally hailed as an important factor in the Soviet "revolution of the military system." [13]

In 1967 the Soviet Chief of Naval Staff, Admiral Gortchkov, referred to methods suggestive of American operational research in a speech explaining the Central Committee's decision to expand the Soviet navy. About the same time a Soviet military journal described instructional air war gaming at the General Staff Academy.[14] It is also possible that the Russians have experimented with mathematical games, whose principles have been explained to Soviet scientific and military audiences in the course of critical descriptions of Western military planning methods.

These developments should be borne in mind when reading the chapters which follow, which deal largely, but not necessarily exclusively, with the pitfalls of military analysis in the West.

[13] Csizmas, *op. cit.*
[14] I. Boikov, "The General Staff Academy," *Soviet Military Review,* Number 6, 1967.

4

POLITICO-MILITARY
GAMES

ONE OF THE PRINCIPAL establishments engaged in war gaming in America is the Joint War Games Agency of the Joint Chiefs of Staff. It is located in the Pentagon and has three divisions. The first, or General War Division, runs strategic war games, including once a year a great game on computers for the U.S. Air Force to test the current defense posture for its response to a hypothetical "Red" attack. The plan of the attack is deliberately varied and is not necessarily the one thought most likely by Air Force Intelligence chiefs. The second division games Limited War, and one of its responsibilities is to test the contingency plans of U.S. commanders-in-chief overseas to see if they are feasible for their purpose. The third division—in many ways the most interesting—is the Cold War Division, which is concerned with the anticipation of high-level crises rather than actual hostilities.

The Cold War Division runs politico-military games, which

could be described as highly developed versions of the games of von Manstein and Japanese war planners before World War II. Their contents are, understandably, secret; but as five or six have been played each year since 1961, one could guess—even without the private confirmation given by participants—that they have explored in advance a fair number of the major and minor international crises encountered by the Kennedy and Johnson administrations. The list has included insurrection in Latin America, communist threats to West Berlin, subversion in northern Thailand, and numerous international complications arising from the war in Vietnam. However, there are two omissions. There was never a game based on Soviet attempts to install nuclear missiles in Cuba (a game was in fact considered in 1962 but was not proceeded with on the grounds that the scenario was too implausible).[1] Nor was there a game based on the possibility of the East Germans building a Berlin wall.

What lends special interest to Cold War Division politico-military games is the status and diversity of the players. These are drawn from almost every branch of the Executive, including the White House, the State Department, the Central Intelligence Agency, and, of course, the Pentagon itself. About three games a year are played at a very senior level, which means on the military side the Joint Chiefs of Staff, and on the civil assistant secretaries, deputy heads of agencies, and the President's national security adviser or his deputy. The

[1] The reasons for its rejection are not hard to understand. As readers of Elie Abel's *The Missiles of October* will be aware, the current strategic appraisal was that the Soviet Union had no motive for installing medium-range missiles in Cuba. The Russians had never installed offensive rockets on any foreign territory, even in the Warsaw Pact countries. Russia, as Khrushchev himself had rightly but disingenuously explained, could police Cuba by means of its own intercontinental ballistic missiles in the Soviet Union; so why should it place them in the hands of a third party with the power to involve it in a thermonuclear war? It did not need the Soviet Ambassador, Mr. Dobrynin, to point this out to Robert Kennedy on September 4th—because the Chiefs of Staff "knew" it already. They did not change their views until the installation of the missiles was confirmed on October 14th.

President and the Secretaries of State and Defense do not attend these Pentagon games, but they receive reports.

Although the Cold War Division is not given to divulging the content of high-level games, there is no secrecy about the method of preparing and conducting them. Preparation is in the hands of seven or eight officers, all with active field experience. Their work begins with the day-to-day study of confidential inter-agency reports. When a game situation suggests itself, it is put up to the Joint Chiefs for approval. The preparation of each game takes about three months. First there are interviews with Joint Staff operations and Intelligence officers, and specialists inside and outside government, particularly in the universities. Next, if the game involves an overseas area, officers fly out to gather information locally and, if possible, arrange for the return of a United States ambassador and other field officers to take part in the game. After this, one officer is assigned to preparing a "fact book" on the area (covering armaments, physical characteristics, technology, resources and so on), while another draws up a paper on "Problems, Issues, and Questions," which is expected to lean heavily on experts with forcefully opposed views. From these and other sources a third officer compiles the game "scenario"—a detailed history of hypothetical events leading up to the crisis situation which the game is to examine. When this is completed, the game teams are assembled.

As a rule each team consists of five to ten players and represents a single country; the maximum number of teams is about seven. Inside teams there is no individual role playing as head of state, chief of staff, and so on. Instead decisions are reached collectively, rather like those of President Kennedy's "executive committee" during the Cuba crisis. The difference between Blue and other teams is that "American" players are free to pursue whatever policy they think best, whereas the others are expected to act in accordance with the recognized ideologies or national attitudes of "their" countries. (How realistically they can do this is a point of interest in politico-military games.) "Our Russian teams," I was told at the Pentagon in 1967, "could play the game in Russian"—which meant that they were largely composed of military Kremlinologists and former ambassadors and military attachés in Moscow.

The playing of a game generally takes three working days. It begins with the presentation of the opening scenario, and proceeds in "cycles" of three to six moves. The essence of each move is a discussion by each team of the options before it. At the end of four hours, often the time that might actually be available for crisis decision making in real life, the team has to decide on its plan, which is normally projected two days to one week ahead in "game time." The outcome of events in the light of each team's plan is decided by a director who, by his interpretation and the occasional interjection of arbitrary events, must carry the scenario forward to the next move. His task is not to be impartial but to steer the game in such a way that attention is kept focused on important issues. For this exacting task directors are generally chosen from the military-academic world outside the Pentagon; and some, such as Thomas Schelling, Albert Wohlstetter, and Lincoln Bloomfield, have acquired a prestige similar to that of umpires like von Meckel and von Trotha in nineteeth-century Prussia. Four-star generals and assistant secretaries do not stay throughout the game but join their teams for two hours a day when critical decisions must be taken. They may, however, keep in touch with their teams by telephone; and at least one chief has been known to break off from the real-life planning of the Vietnam war to ask several times a day how next year's crisis is going in Bolivia.

When the game is ended it is followed by an analysis, and in due course the whole scenario is worked up into a thirty-minute film, enlivened with "actuality" pictures of riots, troop movements, missile firings, and so on, which is shown to selected "policy-making groups" in the Pentagon and State

Department, together with a critical commentary pointing out where Blue may have erred.

The politico-military game was not invented by the Pentagon but by a social scientist at the Rand Corporation, Herbert Goldhamer. In 1954 Goldhamer became interested in the field as a result of attempts to devise a "Cold War game" in which political and economic factors would be given numerical values so that the relative worth of alternative strategies could be quantitatively measured. The attempt was abandoned when it became clear that the simplification involved made it worthless for assessing political strategies in the real world.

Goldhamer, who knew about the Manstein and Tokyo games, suggested a method which, while simpler in itself, offered a better chance to simulate real world complexity. In the game he suggested, the government of each country would be represented by a separate player or team, while another team or player would represent "Nature." The latter's function, which was a novelty in war games, was to provide for events of the kind that happen in the real world but are not subject to government control, for example certain technological developments, the deaths of important people, famines and other "acts of God." In time, however, it was found that this could be better performed by the team of referees, whose main task was to rule on the feasibility of each move.

As in the Pentagon game, Goldhamer's teams were to be area specialists acting as "their" governments would in the prevailing circumstances—except for the American team, which would act freely. The chief difference between the two lay in Goldhamer's purpose. His object was to be able to test a wide range of strategies, and for this it was proposed to play the same situation a number of times, observing the consistency of the outcome and the effect of making alterations in strategy.

In 1955–56 four games were played, the last two being fairly elaborate. All moves were made in writing, and teams had to state their motives and expectations, which the referees could challenge. Some moves were "open" for all to see, while others were "game classified," i.e., secret. But the referees could "leak" the contents of game classified papers, accurately or in distorted form, to other teams, thus simulating the Intelligence function in the political process as well as the deliberate leaking of policy secrets which occurs from time to time in a free press.

The fourth game was focused on the activities of the United States and the Soviet Union in a crisis projected nine months ahead. In three weeks' play 150 papers were written by the participants, who included a number of senior Foreign Service officers as well as members of Rand's Social Science, Economics, and Physics divisions. In addition there were frequent consultations with outside experts whenever the game called for specialist knowledge in fields such as weapons development.

Today Goldhamer, who is still at Rand (involved with the Cold War as a specialist in Latin-American affairs), says that in its original purpose the experiment was a failure. "I realized," he says, "that I had created a Frankenstein monster. To test strategies and forecast political developments would have required each game to be repeated many times. But a single game took months to prepare and weeks to play. And all the players were pretty busy men."

But although this difficulty led the Rand games to be discontinued, they were felt to have yielded some useful experience. For example, although a particular strategy might not be tested by a single game, players *did* become aware of pitfalls and problems that surrounded a strategy. In fact, according to Goldhamer, several developments in the fourth game anticipated developments that occurred later on in real life. The game, he wrote later, "provided a lively setting in which to study the contemporary political world, gave specialists a view outside their own fields, and provided new understanding of the pressures under which foreign policy decisions are made." [2]

The Rand games caused interest, and ultimately imitation, in a wide variety of environments. In the following years Goldhamer and other Rand staff members were invited to lecture at institutions as opposite in character as the Army War College and the Carnegie Endowment for International Peace at Princeton. There were discussions with the State Department, the Brookings Institution, and the Harvard Center for International Affairs. At the Massachusetts Institute of Technology (where a Rand man happened to be a visiting professor) an improved version of Goldhamer's game was developed by Lincoln Bloomfield, who used it to explore questions of arms control policy in a series of exercises for the Institute of Defense Analyses. At Northwestern University it was adopted by Professor Harold Guetzkow as a basis for experimental simulation to study and teach international relations. Finally, in 1961, it was taken up at the Pentagon by the Joint Staff.

Now, the Pentagon politico-military games belong to the "educational" type of game suggested by the Rand experiment. According to the Joint War Games Agency, their function is simply to exercise policy makers in the kind of problem that could face them in a real world crisis. Nobody, it is said, would ever think of setting up a game to predict the success of a particular strategy or policy, as the Japanese did in their games in World War II.

If this is so, the question to be asked is: How well do they educate those who take part?

In 1967 I taxed a dozen game-experienced members of the United States administration and armed forces with this question, and received mixed answers. Broadly speaking, the State Department men were rather skeptical. One said he thought

[2] H. Goldhamer and H. Speier, "Some Observations on Political Gaming," *World Politics*, October 1959.

there were more effective ways of spending one's time. Another said that if the games benefited anybody, it must be the military who, from what he had seen, had plenty to learn about foreign policy problems. But most agreed that so long as games were not used to *predict* future events, they could do no harm, and that possibly they did some good.

The military were more positive. They said games provided "insights" (a much-used word in the games business) into problems whose existence might otherwise have been overlooked. Games, they said, were more likely to expose the dangers of a particular line of action than to provide false grounds for recommending it. They also claimed that games "extended the horizons" of people who were used to working on limited aspects of a problem; that they provided a "showcase" for new ideas which hard-boiled policy makers would otherwise refuse to look at; and that they were a splendid means of getting officials into a "questioning mood" about the existing policies of their departments.

Subsequently I sought the opinion of a game director, Thomas Schelling, at the Harvard Center for International Relations.

Schelling, a thoughtful academic who has directed seven or eight games for the Pentagon (his first was on Berlin in 1961), endorsed what the military had said and added some observations of his own. One thing games could teach, he said, was how little of strategy, or even war, was military; how it was less concerned with the application of force than with the exploitation of *potential* force. They could teach the importance of communicating with one's opponent, not only by what one said but by what one did. At a practical level they could lead to discoveries. For example, there had been a game based on a situation in the Middle East in which one of Blue's problems was a local shortage of aviation fuel— until the Red side decided to stage some fires as a demonstration of a city's instability, and suddenly a CIA man had

realized that domestic kerosene stocks represented a supply
of jet fuel. Schelling said that as a director he had also observed some things about crisis behavior that might not otherwise have come to light. For example, how goals tended to
change in the course of a situation. Thus if things were going
well for a side, there was a tendency to seize opportunities;
but if a side was losing, it tended to forget its original objectives. Another thing he had observed was how when a team
tried to take a bold decision, the other side generally reacted
less than the first team had intended, with the result that the
action turned out to be less bold than intended. One reason
for this seemed to be that every team contained both hawks
and doves; but that the two elements tended to concentrate
on different parts of the situation, the hawks on the remote
contingency, the doves on the near one. The opposing team,
however, judged by what it actually saw, which was the immediate picture. "For example," he explained, "suppose I have
a gun, intending to shoot you if you show disrespect to me;
but you don't show disrespect *this* time. Then you don't see
how bold I am." Schelling thought games could be used to
learn more about this kind of thing, but at present they were
not used systematically enough.

A more systematic analysis than my own random inquiry
had in fact been made two years before among people who
had taken part in politico-military games at the Massachusetts Institute of Technology. It was based on answers to a
questionnaire, in many cases followed by an interview, sent
in by 82 government officials and others who had played in
one or more of a series of eight games similar in character to
Pentagon politico-military games. The government officials
included State Department, Department of Defense, and CIA
men, and a typical game cited was one in 1963 based on
United States policy options following a Chinese invasion
of South Vietnam.

Of the respondents

35.1% said they had learned something about the process of contemporary international relations.

40.2% said they had learned something about foreign policy planning processes.

37.8% said they had learned something about crisis management and decision making in crises.

65.9% said they had gained from the experience "in general." [3]

For research and policy planning purposes in general, the respondents rated the value of the technique of gaming in the following descending order (mean ratings, out of a possible 6.0, in parentheses):

1. for discovering *unanticipated* policy alternatives in international problem situations (4.2);

2. for discovering *unanticipated* possible outcomes of the interaction of conflicting strategies or specific crisis situations (4.1);

3. for *generating* new hypotheses about the nature of crisis management or decision making in crisis situations (4.0);

4. for increasing the precision and effectiveness of the foreign policy planning process (3.8);

5. for *evaluating* the validity and viability of various existing United States policies in international crisis situations (3.8);

6. for *testing* hypotheses about the nature of crisis management or decision making in crisis situations (3.8);

7. for determining the likely *effects* of various possible United States policies in crisis situations (3.7);

8. for *generating* new hypotheses about the structure and process of contemporary international relations (3.6);

9. for *testing* tentative hypotheses about the structure and process of international relations (3.4);

10. for determining the probable *reactions of other actors* to various possible United States policy moves in a specific crisis (3.4).

[3] R. E. Barringer and B. Whaley, "The M.I.T. Politico-Military Gaming Experience," *Orbis*, Summer 1965.

While these statistics tended to confirm that games were *potentially* useful, particularly as a means of stimulating or testing ideas in policy planning, the survey reached some other perhaps cautionary conclusions. For example, that the "insights and lessons taught by a game tend to be largely dependent on the knowledge and preoccupations that a player brings to it." In other words, that "what occurs under the stresses of gaming is not so much something new that is learned as heightened awareness of things previously known." Another conclusion, based on remarks by respondents about the difficulty of grasping scenarios projected several years ahead, was that "a participant brings to any scenario his own assumptions about contemporary reality and tends to use them rather than bear the discomfort and constraint of new, unfamiliar ones." While the authors of the survey saw the use of games for discovering unanticipated possibilities in the international field as perhaps their greatest potential, they also saw it as a possible danger. For although games provided a valuable "feel" for the timing, logistics, and political implications of a crisis, such a familiarization could "restrict a participant's imagination and range of choice in face of a real crisis situation which he saw as analogous." [4]

The M.I.T. survey makes no mention of "prediction," which the Pentagon says has no place in politico-military games. Nevertheless, at least two of the ways in which the M.I.T. respondents saw such games as valuable—namely for "determining the likely effects of various possible United States policies" and "determining the probable reactions of other actors to various possible United States policy moves"— come very close to it. Others, such as "evaluating the validity and viability of various existing United States policies," point to the importance of validity in the games themselves. For if a game misrepresents "real world" conditions, any evaluations

[4] Barringer and Whaley, *op. cit.*

made by the participants will be worthless. This must be particularly important in the case of games played by actual policy makers.

Yet at both the Pentagon and the State Department I detected a tendency to play down the possibility that a game based on false assumptions might mislead policy makers about problems in the real world. Games, it was said, were only one of a variety of ways in which policy makers explored military and foreign relations problems. They could never be a solitary influence on a policy decision, but were inevitably mixed with others such as professional experience, the study of real-world crises, and so on. This happened in such a way that it was impossible to say that one influence was more important than any other. In any case, I was told, politico-military games could never directly influence the highest decision makers, because the President and his senior cabinet members never took part in them.

Now, although in a formal sense this last point is true, it is also misleading. For it implies that Presidential decisions are made in a kind of quarantine through which the germs of ideas hatched in war games cannot pass. In fact, a majority of Pentagon politico-military games involve experts on whom the President or Defense Secretary rely heavily for advice on important matters such as the effect of American troop withdrawals from Europe, the implications of deploying an anti-missile system, and the feasibility of politico-military goals in Southeast Asia. The fact that the President does not take part *directly* may therefore be of small importance. (President Kennedy did in fact play politico-military games with some members of his staff at the White House, but perhaps we should not attach too much importance to these informal exercises, about which, in any case, very little is known.)

As we have seen, some trouble is taken to provide Pentagon politico-military games with realistic, factual scenarios. But there are numerous ways in which the playing of them can

POLITICO-MILITARY GAMES ∦ 75

present a false picture. For example, since teams work as one unit, they have no internal problem of command and control. Also, since the game is a make-believe, there may be a tendency to resort to harsh actions with fewer qualms than in real life. Another unrealistic feature is the absence of domestic political considerations to interfere with policy decisions. A fourth point, made to me by some State Department men, is that in real life you seldom have a single crisis to deal with but several simultaneously. All these unrealities are accepted as the price of "isolating" the problem under study, and, in theory at least, are remembered in the subsequent analysis.

But there is one area in which all games are open to the danger of unrealism in a way that can have serious consequences. This is in the playing of Red.

It requires great subtlety of mind to get beneath the skin of one's opponent. It may be relatively easy for a commander in a battle, when terrain, the known performance of weapons, and certain general tactical principles, provide both sides with a common frame of reference. But when the picture is enlarged—from a battle to a campaign, and a campaign to a war—more and more factors are involved about which the opposing sides may have quite different concepts. To assume the personality of one's opponent in a politico-military crisis, where major questions of national temperament, philosophy, and value judgment are involved, may be very difficult indeed. This is what Red players in a crisis game must do.

Moreover, to play Red with fidelity requires more than just a knowledge of the real Red's attitude with regard to his own plans and actions. It also means knowing how the real Red sees Blue, which may be very different from the way Blue sees himself. This in turn requires knowing the real Red's picture of Blue's picture of Red, and so on *ad infinitum*. In practice, playing Red is like standing between two distorting mirrors and trying to make out a series of increasingly confused reflections. The ability to do this might be found in an Intelligence officer who has identified himself so closely with his real-life opponents as to adopt their philosophy. But such officers are not easily found in the Pentagon war game room. "How can you be sure that we don't have a subversive playing Red?" a visiting general once asked apprehensively during a game. "Don't worry," said a member of the directing staff, "we've been trying to get hold of one for years."

It is not Red's private difficulties that matter, but their effect on the course of the game. If he plays on assumptions that would be quite foreign to the real Red, the purpose of the exercise will be defeated. For either Blue will "get away with" strategic solutions that would fail in real life, or he will be encouraged to discard reasonable solutions and resort to others which may be extravagant or dangerous. While this may not be serious on isolated occasions, it will be serious if it happens consistently. Moreover, it may involve two kinds of error—errors of information and those which could be called errors of insight. Errors of information concern theoretically observable matters such as the state of Red's technology and the balance of political forces in his country. Errors of insight involve failure to comprehend Red's national aspirations or political ideology, in other words, his system of values.

The accuracy of information affecting Red's military and technological status is something over which the organizers of politico-military games have little control. In preparing scenarios and briefing players they have access to recent Intelligence estimates by the National Security Agency and the CIA. (Hence all participants, inside or outside government, must have a high security grading.) But they can do nothing to improve this information, which may often be seriously wrong, as it was about the Soviet "missile lead" until the defection of the Soviet agent Oleg Penkovsky in 1961. Errors of insight are something a well-conducted game might cure; but whether this happens depends largely on the ability of the director.

In the case of Red's attitude towards Blue a quite different kind of Intelligence problem arises. As we saw, Pentagon

"Russian" teams include former military attachés and Moscow-based diplomats who may bring to their role a useful knowledge of the practical workings of the Soviet politico-military system. But such players also have information about the working of the *American* system, including contingency plans, which would not, optimistically, be available to real Soviet policy makers; and unless they can forget it (which is a practical impossibility) their play may be quite unauthentic.

The problem might have seemed rather theoretical had it not come to light in a discussion I had at another war game "workshop," the nongovernmental Stanford Research Institute, which, among other activities, does operational research under contract to the Army.

The S.R.I. games, being conducted for research purposes, are in some ways more meticulously prepared than politico-military ones. For example, the Institute keeps a "back room" full of experts working continuously on the study of the Soviet economy, technology, military doctrine, and so forth in order to provide a supply of "instant Red" in war games. These games are used to determine the future direction of Soviet arms policy as a preliminary to making cost comparisons of envisaged future weapons systems—new nuclear warheads, missile penetration aids, decoys, etc.—in both the United States and the Soviet Union. But they pose the inevitable question, how much do Soviet decision makers know, or guess, about American arms policy when formulating their own? To deal with this the Institute has evolved an incontrovertibly safe solution. It divides its Red research team into two sections. One section, working under tight security, has full access to classified information about American plans; the other works in physical separation without access to secrets of any kind. When the time comes to set up a game, the game (or series) is played twice: first on the assumption that Red has *all* Blue's secrets, when the "classified" team plays; then on the assumption that it has none, when the other team plays. The separate outcomes are then taken as the extremes between which reality lies.

When I raised the question of the Stanford games with an officer who had been closely involved with Pentagon games, he pointed out that to double-play educational games in this way would merely give the players in each performance a totally unrealistic exercise. He also pointed out that to attempt to play Red with exactitude would be self-defeating, because politico-military games are invariably projected at situations in the future. In these circumstances a successful simulation of the current Red attitudes could be misleading. "Suppose," he said, "that we had had Khrushchev himself playing Red in some game two years ago. What guide would it have been to what Kosygin might do in the same situation tomorrow?" When I asked why, in that case, an effort was made to "act" Red at all, I was told that only by working within the framework of constraints and compulsions in Red's system could one gain an insight into the options which would be open to him in some hypothetical future.

This is an argument frequently made for role playing in politico-military games. But it contains a circular proposition —"Red's choice of action can be learned by examining Blue's choices, which can be learned by examining Red's"—as well as resting on the assumption that the constraints and compulsions in Red's system can actually be known. The evidence against this is substantial. For even in considering a political system close to their own, Western policy makers may dramatically fail to appreciate the effect of their actions—as shown by American surprise at the reaction of the British Macmillan government to the cancellation of Skybolt in 1962.

Doubts about the ability of American game players to put on the mantle of communist thought exist even among members of the American strategic community, as I found in a conversation with an American Kremlinologist, Robert Dickson Crane.

I met Crane at another military-analytical establishment, the Hudson Institute. When I mentioned the Stanford games, Crane said that any attempt to create "synthetic Russians" was bound to fail because American and Soviet policy makers simply did not think the same way. He pointed to the complicated role of dialectical materialism in Soviet military thinking, and to the Marxist rejection of the Western concept of an objective military science not based on any political philosophy. Since Russia's setback in the Cuba crisis, he said, a new generation of Soviet military theorists had been invoking dialectical materialism as a new source of guidance. "You might see it as an attempt on their part to create an authority independent of the Party to which to appeal for more flexible and realistic thinking." These "new" theorists were repeatedly emphasizing that dialectical materialism offered a means of understanding the process of change, and the possibilities inherent in it, so that military science could stay ahead of the mere study of past events. At the same time the most pervasive influence on Soviet policy was the basic Marxist-Leninist teaching that conflict is not necessarily evil but a valuable instrument for progress. The American "elite," he asserted, could never grasp this view, at least when their eyes were fixed on comprehensive East-West agreements. They believed that to any rational government stability and the resolution of conflict were self-evident desirable goals; whereas to the Russians the logical goal was "managed instability"—in other words, the Russians believed that within the limits required by minimum world stability, conflict should be promoted.

Now it could be argued that although games are susceptible to errors of the kind we have described, they can also draw attention to the need to correct them in actual policy making. But here the observer can hardly be blamed if he turns for evidence to the record of United States policy to which politico-military games have been contributing for seven years.

The results are not very promising. It is true that nuclear war has been avoided, and also that for five years there has been no attempt to threaten the security of the United States on its home ground. This may be due, in part, to the strategy of deterrence, in whose formulation gaming has played a part. But politico-military gaming has clearly not prevented the kind of mistake that it is supposed to. For example, it has not stopped a tendency to take a limited number of possibly quite valid assumptions, such as the "domino theory" in Southeast Asia, and suppose them to be the only ones that matter. Nor has it prevented a failure to recognize how limited an achievement may be, e.g., victory in Vietnam, even if it comes off. Nor has it stopped a tendency to state plausible outcomes tentatively, then to forget that they are tentative, with the result that there is a gradual but irreversible escalation.

The observer may also be struck by the thought that the Cuban crisis, which was never gamed beforehand, was more effectively solved than many subsequent crises which games anticipated.

It is possible, of course, that we are blaming the *technique* of politico-military gaming for failures which lie more with the way in which it has been practiced. It may be that but for politico-military gaming there would have been even more errors in American external policy than there have been, though the chapter of troubles stemming from Vietnam makes this hard to believe. But two things are not disputed, even by those who believe that politico-military games may serve a useful purpose. No amount of gaming, however well conducted, can ever uncover the future. Nor can it supply decision makers, if they do not already have it in them, with the vital element in decision making which Clausewitz called "tact." To suppose either of these things is to perpetuate the belief that given enough resources and organization, every politico-military problem can be solved. It is this belief which partly accounts for the vast investment of skill and resources in the games described in the succeeding chapters.

5

TACTICIANS IN THE LABORATORY

THE GAMES with which we shall now be concerned are in the literal sense *war* games, whose connection with politico-military games may be found by inverting Clausewitz' dictum that war is a continuation of politics with the "admixture of other means." In spite of the sophistication brought to them by modern electronics, war games remain what they were in the nineteenth century: attempts to represent in the neatness of the laboratory the bloodiness and mess of the field. They continue to serve the same purposes—instruction, the analysis of military problems, the testing of strategies and plans—to which has been added another: the selection of new weapons systems.

One type of war game in the fullest sense of the term (it is used to study a whole war rather than a battle situation) is the "hot war" equivalent of the politico-military game. A prototype of this kind of game was developed at the Rand

81

Corporation in 1954 as part of a "limited war" study called Project Sierra. Envisaging wars two to five years ahead in Southeast Asia and the Middle East, each series of Sierra games began with a "curtain-raiser." In this, Red was given the chance to prepare and conduct military operations against Blue in face of a very restricted response. This was to set a a "realistic" scene for the subsequent five or six games, each of which explored the effects of a more active type of response. The games, according to a Rand paper, provided useful information about the advantages and limitations of various military postures; a comparison of the utility of various weapons, including nuclear, bacteriological, and chemical weapons; and light on "uncertainties in the planning, conduct, and termination of future military operations." [1]

By comparison with this the modern type of tactical war game, often still played like the games of von Reisswitz, on a map or "board," might seem simpler. But the situation which the tactical game is required to represent is in fact very complex. It concludes the interactions between two sides or, more exactly, the influence of each side's weapons and tactics on the other side's weapons and tactics, and the influence on both of factors such as ground and weather. Plainly an alteration in the character of any one of these elements has an effect, directly or indirectly, on one or more of the others. It also includes the way in which each commander controls, or tries to control, the battle, on the basis of information about his own troops and intelligence about the enemy's.

In the commonest type of tactical war game—the so-called closed type—the Blue and Red commanders are isolated in separate rooms. Each has a physical model, in some cases simply a map, of the ground on which the battle is to take place. Symbols representing men and weapons are placed on this model in accordance with the commander's plan. There is

---

[1] M. G. Weiner, "An Introduction to War Games" (mimeo). The Rand Corporation, Santa Monica, Calif., 1959.

also a control room containing a similar model, on which the positions of both sides' symbols are duplicated. Moves by Red and Blue are relayed to this room and appropriate adjustments made to the pieces. The outcome of the moves is then determined by rules in the case of a rigidly assessed game and by the umpire's judgment in a free one. Some rules may be absolute, for example those governing speed of movement. Others are "probabilistic," i.e., assigning some latitude to the outcome of an event and leaving it to a dicelike device, sometimes called a Monte Carlo machine, to decide the exact result. According to the outcome, the pieces are again adjusted and information and intelligence, including a realistic amount of doubtful information, is passed to the players to provide the basis for the next move cycle.

A typical modern tactical game is played at the U.S. Marine Corps Landing Force Development Center at Quantico, Virginia. Anyone tempted to dismiss such "mere tactical" games as of minor importance in international developments should consider the regularity with which the Marines are dispatched on fire-brigade missions in support of American policy around the globe. Since the end of World War II they have performed thirty-one such missions, ranging from the commitment of a single battalion to suppress civil war in a Latin-American neighbor, the Dominican Republic, to the landing of a complete Marine division in Lebanon.

The Landing Force War Game—the only war game used by the Marines—has been played at Quantico, virtually without a break, since 1958, when it was developed from a war game devised by the Canadian army. Sometimes the scene is set in Latin America, sometimes in Southeast Asia, sometimes in the Middle East. (Cyprus is a popular setting because of the excellence of the survey maps produced by the British in their war with General Grivas.) The Red forces vary from primitively armed guerrillas to sophisticated opponents with armor, artillery, and tactical air power. Only one feature is permanent: the Blue forces are always Marines, a fact which contains numerous assumptions including the traditional one that "the Marines never quit."

When I visited Quantico in 1967 two Marine lieutenant colonels were playing a game to analyze the helicopter requirements of a Marine division. The game board was a map of Cuba, about 20 by 40 feet, occupying the center of the control room. Red and Blue symbols sprouted profusely, their shape and size—square, triangular, and cylindrical—denoting different types of unit. Some blocks, headquarter units, had pins through the center, enabling support unit pieces to be superimposed on them. There were also colored pins to mark minefields, destroyed bridges, and evacuated positions which might still appear occupied to reconnaissance aircraft. At one end of the board a stout desk supported two thick volumes of the rule book.

The Landing Force War Game is a rigidly assessed "closed" game. Moves are made at game-time intervals of between thirty minutes and several days; but because of the work of moving pieces, determining results, and writing up a game diary for later analysis, a game covering twenty to thirty hours of action generally takes about four months to complete.

In the game in question Blue forces had landed in the north of the island, and, having captured the provincial capital of Pinar del Río, were advancing with Havana as the objective. Both Marine Corps tanks and fighter bombers were engaged, and the outcome of every clash was determined by a Monte Carlo device called a random number generator. This is the modern counterpart of von Reisswitz' dice and consists of thermionic valve circuits designed to produce ten different wave patterns at random. When a key is pressed the pattern being generated at that instant causes a decimal digit to appear on the face of a cathode ray tube. At Quantico the apparatus showed digits in pairs so that when, for example, the rules laid down a 30-percent probability of one tank knocking out another at a specified range, any number between 00 and 29 would indicate a "kill," while numbers between 30 and 99 showed "no-kill." The machine was also used to decide which side fired first in certain encounters, whether certain radio links were working, and whether air reconnaissance correctly interpreted the status of enemy positions.

The Blue and Red commanders received information in the form of situation reports, Intelligence digests, aerial photographic interpretations, and so on. Their moves took the form of written orders to subordinate units and reports to the higher command. The Red colonel worked beneath a framed picture of Fidel Castro; the Blue beneath a placard which said "Remember it's only a game." They had been fighting each other for several weeks and did not, I gathered, meet much in the mess any more.

The Landing Force War Game is extremely flexible. It can be focused on a landing of battalion size or expanded to represent complete divisional operation. Sometimes it is used for training, sometimes to examine new concepts or requirements. When attention is fixed on a particular item, the relevant sections of the rule book can be expanded to permit the detailed variation of factors affecting it, e.g., changes in visibility in the case of a game to evelute the requirement for additional reconnaissance aircraft. Similarly sections can be "aggregated," making it possible, say, to determine the outcome of a company-sized ground action in a single move instead of working out the effect of each shot. Normally commanders have freedom of action such as they would expect in the field. Blue can do what he likes so long as he observes Marine Corps doctrine, and Red so long as he observes the limits imposed by the structure of the national force he represents. But in so-called *operational* war gaming, whose purpose is to test contingency plans, Blue must follow the existing operation order prepared and filed at command headquarters.

A larger kind of tactical game is played at the United Kingdom Defence Operational Analysis Establishment at Byfleet,

Surrey. DOAE's war-gaming activities are in some respects similar to those of the Limited War division of the U.S. Joint War Games Agency, though cynics might observe that whereas the JWGA has been active in exploring new fields for military action, DOAE has largely been engaged in finding ways of trimming the British defense effort to a minimum. Among the subjects gamed at Byfleet have been the capability of British forces "east of Suez" and the duration of the resistance that Allied forces could offer to a Soviet invasion of Western Europe.

Since the early 1960s DOAE has played a whole series of "Corps games" in which a British corps fights an unequal battle with up to two Soviet armies. Each game takes between six and eight weeks, representing about three days of "real time" fighting. The commanders on either side are generally brigadiers or major generals on temporary attachment between postings—a practice intended to ensure that the sides are realistically commanded and that the usefulness of gaming is impressed on future Army commanders.

The terrain model in these games is a relief model divided into two-kilometer squares, and represents an area of 150 by 90 kilometers overall. The symbols represent units of company size, but for convenience both integration and division of pieces is possible. In a typical game there are 1,000–2,000 pieces on the control board. A game cycle represents one hour of battle time. During each cycle each commander relays orders concerning fire and movement to Control. After assessing any interactions between the two sides, Control gives each side the relevant intelligence. The controllers are bound by the rule book and only in very exceptional circumstances are they allowed to use their own judgment, generally to ensure that a correct military interpretation is given to the game situation that has occurred. The rules of the DOAE tactical war game are very detailed and are said to cover all foreseeable situations. They occupy a book of 100 foolscap pages and are based on the results of past operations, scientific assessment, and data obtained from field trials and exercises. Communications between Control and the commanders are mainly by radio and telephone, but these are backed up by teleprinters. Some voice communications are recorded and later transcribed. During the actual game a staff of about twenty is employed, of whom about a third are military officers. The normal target is to play fifteen cycles a week. In 1965 the cost of running the game was about £50,000 a year.

Another type of game at DOAE is used to study the supply problems of a British corps in Germany in time of war. Ports and supply lines are represented on a network model, over which are moved pieces representing ships, road convoys, and so on. Loading and marshaling times are included, as well as delays due to enemy action. Blue's command room is amalgamated with the control room since it is assumed that the Blue commander has full intelligence of the situation. But the Red commander, in a separate room, is only given intelligence that he might receive in real life from air reconnaissance, agents, and other intelligence sources. On the basis of this he plans countermeasures such as sea mining and air attack.

A number of Byfleet tactical games have been concerned with tactical nuclear doctrine in NATO and one of these is well documented.[2] It was played about 1960 and represented a battle between three NATO corps and numerically superior forces attacking across the German zonal border. The scenario envisaged a resort to tactical nuclear weapons against military targets only. The area of the battle was approximately 10,000 square miles and included no large towns or cities. In it the two sides were assumed to use a total of between twenty and twenty-five megatons in not fewer than 500 and not more than 1,000 strikes. The game revealed that three and a half million people would have had their homes destroyed if the weapons had been airburst, and one and a half million if

2 S. Zuckerman, "Judgment and Control in Modern Warfare," *Foreign Affairs*, 40:196–212, January 1962.

they had been ground-burst. In the former case at least half the people concerned would have been fatally or seriously injured. In the case of ground-burst weapons, all one and a half million would have been exposed to a lethal radiological hazard and a further five million to serious danger from radiation. This, moreover, took no account of civilian casualties from the nuclear strikes at tactical missile locations and lines of communication which would inevitably have accompanied the local nuclear battle. The outcome of the game caused the British government's chief defense adviser, then Sir Solly Zuckerman, to ask searching—and still unanswered —questions about the ability of military commanders to exercise judgment and control in the chaos following an unrestrained nuclear exchange, in which 15,000 tactical nuclear warheads would be available to the Allied forces alone.

Now all the games described above are "manual." From the military-technical point of view they have certain advantages compared with more sophisticated types. They are relatively faithful in their representation of complicated situations. They employ human actors whose thought processes cannot be simulated mechanically. They include the element of chance, which is an essential ingredient in war. And those who design them are supposed to become quickly aware of potentially critical parts of a situation about which there may be little or no data. But one of their chief drawbacks, as the technicians see it, is the time they take to play.

A highly mechanized type of game, which partly overcomes this difficulty, has been developed at the U.S. Naval War College at Newport, Rhode Island. It is played on a vast apparatus called the Navy Electronic War Simulator (NEWS), which occupies a whole building including an auditorium in which observers and control staff can watch the progress of the battle. Instead of a maneuver board there is an illuminated screen on which the symbols for ships, submarines, and aircraft are electromechanically projected. An electronic weapon-and-damage computer takes the place of computing tables and measuring instruments, and the laborious writing of signals is replaced by an electronic communications system.

The players operate in twenty command rooms, each furnished with charts, plotting screens, fire control panels, and other paraphernalia of a ship's fighting bridge. Connected with the command rooms are rows of electronic units for programming the movements of each of the forty-eight vessels or aircraft that can be represented in the game, together with devices for simulating electronic countermeasures, malfunctions of weapons, and the susceptibility of any unit to radar or sonar detection.

I watched a game in which a carrier task force maneuvered for attack against a hostile port. The action developed on the big central screen, lit from behind with ultraviolet light. The auditorium was in darkness except for small lamps above the desks of the control staff. On each side of the screen were columns of illuminated panels showing the status of every unit in the two engaged forces, which for esoteric naval reasons are designated Green and White. Other devices showed the course, depth, or altitude of each fighting unit and banks of small lights indicated the status of each unit's weapons, whether active or nonfunctioning. When a Green unit acquired a White target, a light would appear in the appropriate White target panel. Then, when the weapons were fired, the light would start flashing, an "under attack" bell would ring in White's control room, and on impact an electronically controlled "kill meter" would register the reduction in White's effectiveness.

An essential component of the NEWS is the game clock, set above the control screen and connected with similar clocks in each command room. This can be driven at 5, 10, 20, or 40 times the speed of "real time." It is also possible to switch the NEWS for play on four different "ocean sizes," ranging from 40 to 4,000 nautical miles square. Changes in time and scale are automatically digested by computers which plot the movement of units on the screen. This enables the game to be focused on details of one part of the action or expanded to take in a broader picture. It is thus possible to play the several types of game that we encountered in Little's day.

For half the year the NEWS is used purely for training purposes, simulating battle for officers on the War College command course. For the rest it is given over to the playing of so-called Fleet games. In these the players are generally an admiral and his staff, in the role of task force or task group commanders. The flying of aircraft, steering of ships, firing of weapons, and so on is taken over by members of the control staff, who report to their game superiors as they would in action. By this means the admiral can do what he could not do at sea; he can speed up or slow down the action, stop it to make evaluations, go back and try different approaches, and expend vast quantities of expensive munitions—including ships.

Fleet games are used to rehearse maneuvers before going to sea, to try out new operational concepts, and to test battle plans. The most ambitious ever played was in 1962, when a "remote play" link was established between Newport and the operational headquarters of the Pacific Fleet air element at Quonset Point. The forces used were those that would be available to the Quonset commander on mobilization. The commander transmitted his order through "secure" communications channels. The Newport staff acted as the enemy, maneuvered the forces, transmitted reports, and injected into the game such environmental factors as weather, sonar conditions, and trawler and merchant traffic. The game simulated 300 hours of operations and enabled the commander to prepare his War Plan in four six-hour days of play.

There are other so-called machine-assisted games which employ electronic apparatus to speed up the manual process. One, known as TACSPIEL, is used for analysis of land-war tactics at division and lower levels. It is played on 1:25,000 scale maps on which are placed colored symbols similar to those we have seen in other war games. Information about each move is punched on cards. These are fed into a computer which assesses the outcome and performs record-keeping functions. In this way the assessment of a move that represents about half an hour of "real time" takes about eight hours to complete. TACSPIEL is used by civilian analysts, who design the game to be played, act as assessors and conduct the analysis. The military element is said to be "injected . . . by retired military officers who act as consultants and players." [4]

A much more elaborate game is THEATERSPIEL, designed by the same organization, the Research and Analysis Corporation. THEATERSPIEL is used by the Army to study problems of employment, strength, structure and support requirements at "theater level." It employs back-projection screens to display the game situation in three separate rooms —Blue, Red, and Control. Players receive intelligence from the control group on the basis of which to prepare operation orders. These are passed back to the appropriate Control section which translates them, as far as possible, into a form that can be handled by a computer. The computer then assesses the outcome of the situation and prints two reports: a casualty assessment report based on its assessment of interacting ground, air, and support operations, and a "master status report" showing the latest position, strength, and supply situation of all units. The control group combines this information with its own assessment of the situation, including the results of guerrilla activity, actions by small units and politico-military developments. Finally, at the end of about three days' work, it issues intelligence reports for the next 24-hour game cycle.

Although these games involve the use of computers, they

[4] F. J. McHugh, "Fundamentals of War Gaming," 3rd edition (mimeo), Newport, R.I., U.S. Naval War College, 1966.

should not be confused with the computer games described in the next chapter. They are still basically manual games, in which all operational decisions (and parts of the assessment) are made by human players on the spot. Machines are confined to relatively simple processes such as computing fire-exchange outcomes and record keeping.

The manual game has great advantages from the point of view of realism. But it presents the technicians with a problem when used for research. For a single "play" of a manual game is inevitably a hit-or-miss affair. It can show (if the initial assumptions are right) that some formula works or that it does not. But it cannot show what would be the *optimum* formula in terms of how to achieve the maximum result with a given quantity of resources, or a given objective with the minimum quantity of resources. To do this, or to make any statistical analysis, it is necessary to play a whole series of games, identically formulated or containing graduated variations of this or that factor. But this is extremely difficult with manual games, not only because of the time they take (even if reduced to a few hours) but also because of the virtual impossibility of exact replication. For even if it were possible to play more than one game with the same players, the players themselves would undergo changes of style and outlook as a result of increasing familiarity with the game situation.

The limits of the manual game began to be felt in the early 1950s when the variety of new weapons becoming available, and the speed with which operational requirements changed, faced military planners with a bewildering variety of choices. Which systems should be adopted to meet the threats of tomorrow as well as those of today? How should they be deployed? How should they be mixed? How could they be integrated with the overall military structure?

Faced with these questions, the planners were attracted to mathematical bases on which to rest or justify their answers. For if, in the case of competing systems, the cost could be accurately stated on one side, and the effectiveness of a system in some quantified way on the other, the problem of choice would be greatly simplified.

In some cases the statistical data required to frame the choice in this way could be obtained from conventional research techniques—the observation of field trials, etc. But where such observations were impossible or inadequate, another means beckoned in the form of war games that were both rigidly assessed and rigidly played, that is to say, games in which the combatants made no command decisions of their own but based every move on calculations from codified rules. For if such games could be devised, the place of human players could be taken by machines entirely. There would be no variations of playing style. And the elimination of the manpower problem, plus the speed of the electronic computing process, would make possible an almost unlimited number of replications.

Historically this development took place during the Eisenhower administration when the various American armed services, each employing its own back-room army of scientists, enjoyed considerably greater independence than they do today. There was thus an incentive to perfect techniques which could be used to back up the budgetary demands of a particular service against those of its rivals. In particular all three major services—Army, Navy, and Air Force—were forward in claiming advantages for rival nuclear delivery systems. However, the real application of systems analysis, in which computer gaming plays an essential part, was reserved for the arrival of the Kennedy administration in 1961. It was then taken over by Robert McNamara and applied without mercy to eliminating projects that could not show a high degree of "cost effectiveness," and to suppressing the competition between services for funds. We shall examine some opinions about the effect of systems analysis in Chapter 8.

But to understand the nature of the machine on which systems analysis relies, we should go back and look at the origins of the computer itself.

6

COMPUTER WAR
GAMES

THE EARLIEST FORM of computer was the abacus, whose use
was observed by Herodotus among the Egyptians. The
Spaniards found it in Mexico, and a fifteenth-century Chinese
version caught the attention of Seki Kowa, the Japanese
"Newton," who added refinements.

But before calculation (and war) could become automated,
it was necessary to develop mathematics. It was not until the
sixteenth century that Stevinius, the Quartermaster General
of William of Orange, evolved a decimal notation for frac-
tions, and the seventeenth that a Scotsman, John Napier, invented logarithms and a primitive calculator called Napier's
bones. In 1642 Blaise Pascal, the son of a French tax collector,
invented the first adding machine, using weighted ratchets to
turn a series of clocks. About one hundred and thirty years
later his invention was improved upon by Leibniz, who used
a cylindrical drum with stepped teeth to produce a device

that could also multiply. After this, progress halted for want of manufacturing precision. But in 1810 an Alsatian, Charles Thomas of Colmar, produced a marketable apparatus. About 1,500 of Thomas' type of machine were made in the next sixty years, until an Englishman, F. J. Baldwin, patented a variant of the Leibniz wheel, which became the ingredient of many desk calculators today.

Now, so far as their product goes—answers to sums—the desk calculator, the modern electronic computer, the abacus, and the ledger clerk all perform the same service. Given unlimited time, the most complex modern war games could be played using any of them.[1] But the essence of much modern war gaming is speed. To provide the information necessary for systems planning it is necessary to game the same situation, with slight variations, many hundreds or thousands of times. To this the electronic process is essential.

The "father" of the high-speed computer was Charles Babbage, a Cambridge professor of mathematics who died in 1871 at the age of eighty. In 1812 Babbage conceived the idea of a "Difference Engine" for calculating logarithmic tables. He demonstrated a small version of the machine to the Royal Society in 1822, but before proceeding much further with its development was taken up with a more ambitious project which he called the Analytical Machine. It was to be "universal," i.e., capable of doing any kind of calculation whatsoever, and also automatic: that is to say, capable of performing a whole series of operations in a fixed sequence by means of a "control unit." The other main units of the machine were to be a store or memory for holding numbers, a "mill" for per-

1 In their excellent book *Electronic Computers* (Penguin Books, 1965) to which I am here much indebted, Hollingdale and Tootill describe a contest staged in 1946 between Private T. N. Wood of the Finance Disbursing Section of the U.S. Army, who was elected by a preliminary competition as the most skilled desk machine operator in Japan, and Kiyoshi Matsuzaki, of the Savings Bureau of the Ministry of Postal Administration. Wood used an electric desk calculating machine and Matsuzaki an abacus. The contest covered five types of calculation involving four basic arithmetic operations, each being judged on speed and accuracy. The result was a victory for Matsuzaki by four to one.

forming the arithmetical operations, and separate units for putting in numbers and instructions at one end, and for displaying the results at the other.

To control the operation Babbage planned a system of punched cards like that used in the Jacquard pattern-weaving process. One set of cards would control the mill, specifying the operation to be carried out (addition, multiplication, etc.); the other would control the transfer of numbers between the mill and the store, achieved by a system of gears and rods. The store was to consist of columns of wheels, each able to rest in any one of ten positions to register a decimal digit.

Babbage was visited in his workrooms by the Duke of Wellington; but there is no hint that the Duke ever suspected the awesome military applications of the Analytical Machine. In any case, like most of Babbage's projects, it was never completed; our knowledge of it comes largely from the notes of Lady Lovelace, the daughter of Lord Byron, who devised what would now be called the *programs,* or schedules of instructions, to enable it to carry out an automatic sequence of calculations. Shortly after Babbage's death, the punched card system was adopted by Herman Hollerith to process the results of the 1880 American census and became the basis of modern card data processing. But it was another half century before another American, Howard Aiken, used the punched card technique to produce, in 1937, the Automatic Sequence Controlled Calculator—the realization of Babbage's dream and mechanical forerunner of the electronic computer.

In the ASCC, as in the Analytical Machine, numbers were stored in registers of ten sets of wheels. Each wheel could assume ten positions and so store one decimal digit. Each group of wheels was mounted on, but not fixed to, a continuously rotating shaft. Any wheel could be connected to the shaft for any desired part of a revolution by an electromagnetic clutch. A brush wiping over ten contacts was fitted to each wheel to show its position electrically. Addition was effected by making appropriate connections between the brushes of one set of wheels and the clutch mechanisms of another, causing the latter to rotate by amounts depending on the number stored in the first set.

The ASCC was a cumbrous affair. It contained three quarters of a million parts and used 500 miles of wire. It took what would now be considered the inordinately long time of three tenths of a second to add two numbers, and four seconds to perform a multiplication. But it stayed in continuous use for about fifteen years.

Under pressure of military requirements the ASCC was followed two years later by the first electronic computer, ENIAC (Electronic Numerical Integrator and Calculator), which used thermionic valves to eliminate moving parts and to perform in an hour what took the ASCC more than a week. ENIAC used a circuit called a ring counter, the electronic equivalent of a counter wheel. The circuit had ten different states, in each of which one out of ten similar valves conducted current. When a pulse was received by the circuit, the valve which was "on" was put off and the next valve put on. When the ninth valve was put off and the valve 0 put on, a signal was given to effect a "carry." In all, some 18,000 valves were employed, and the malfunction of any one of them had a disastrous effect on the computer's efficiency. ENIAC's other limitations were its small storage capacity and the difficulty of changing from one problem to another, which involved unplugging and rearranging numerous electrical leads. Nevertheless, it was used for many years, for purposes far beyond its immediate one—the calculation of artillery shell and bomb trajectories.

The modern electronic computer, which superseded ENIAC, was the result of ideas worked out by a group of mathematicians and engineers led by the American mathematician John von Neumann, whom we shall encounter later in the different context of Game Theory. It can still be regarded as the electronic replica of Babbage's machine and contains the same basic units—an input and an output unit, a control unit, an arithmetic unit (Babbage's "mill"), and a storage unit, or "memory," for numbers and instructions. Its chief difference from ENIAC is in the manner of counting. For whereas ENIAC, like most human arithmeticians, used the decimal system of counting, the modern computer counts not in tens but in twos.

This is illustrated by the following table in which the left hand column represents a sequence of decimal numbers and the right hand their equivalents in the binary system used by the computer.

0	0000
1	0001
2	0010
3	0011
4	0100
5	0101
6	0110
7	0111
8	1000
9	1001
10	1010
11	1011
12	1100
13	1101
14	1110
15	1111

The reason for the adoption of the binary system is that the most convenient way of storing a number electronically has been found to be by means of a small ring of ferromagnetic material called a core. When a current is passed along a wire through the hole in the ring, the ring becomes magnetized and remains so. A current passed in the opposite direction causes the core to be magnetized in the opposite direction. By this means the direction of the magnetization can be used to represent either of two digits: zero or one.

In a modern computer the cores, about 0.05 inches in

diameter, are threaded like tiny beads on two sets of wires. The first set, called "write" wires, is used to magnetize the cores. The second, called "read" wires, is for reading whether the stored digit is a zero or a one, an answer obtained from variations in the voltage when a current is passed through the wire.

Each group of cores designed to store a number is known as an "address." There are also cores in what is called the "accumulator." The accumulator is the heart of the arithmetic unit, which otherwise consists of a set of so-called "logical circuits." These are designed to pass an electric current along a certain route when one condition exists in the system, to interrupt it (or pass it along a different route) in the case of another condition.

The way in which the computer performs an addition is best explained by a simplified example. Let us suppose that it is required to add 4 and 6, and that 4 is lodged as the binary number 0100 in an address which we shall call A, and 6 as the binary number 0110 in an address we shall call B. Let us also suppose that there are four cores in the accumulator, designated in Figure 1 by the bracketed figures [1], [2], [3], and [4].

The instruction given to the control unit for the operation will be something like:

> Write the number in address A in the accumulator.
> Write the number in the address B in the accumulator.
> Write the contents of the accumulator in address C.

In response to the first command the control unit—reading the number in address A (0100)—causes a magnetic state equivalent to the digit 0 to be induced in cores [1], [3], and [4] of the accumulator, and a state equivalent to the digit 1 to be induced in core [2].

In response to the second command, the unit—reading the number in address B (0110)—causes the state equivalent to 0 to be superimposed, as it were, on cores [1] and [4] and that of 1 on cores [2] and [3]. But due to the designs of the logical circuits, this does not mean erasing the first magnetic state and substituting the second. Instead, where 1 is imposed on 0 and *vice versa,* a "1" results; where 0 is imposed on 0, a "0" results; and where 1 is imposed on 1 (because we are counting in binary numbers) a "0" is produced and a step made equivalent to carrying 1 to the next column. However, unlike the procedure in manual sums, the arithmetic unit does not carry such "bits"—as binary digits are called—individually, but puts them into a carry line, physically consisting of further cores, for adding in as a whole at the end of the sum.

In response to the third command, the control unit in our example reads the result in the accumulator—which, as the reader can check, is the binary equivalent of 10—and causes the same figure to be written in address C. The accumulator is simultaneously "wiped clean" for the next operation.

In addition to its basic mathematical functions (subtraction may be performed by adding complements of numbers and multiplication by a process of repeated addition) the arithmetic unit can compare two numbers in the same way that a war-game umpire compares random numbers with hit probabilities assigned by the game rules. The unit, according to instructions, then decides to take the next prescribed step or to branch to another step.

	[1]	[2]	[3]	[4]	
	0	1	0	0	(transferred from address A)
(transferred from B)	0	1	1	0	
	0	0	1	0	
Carry Line	1				
	1	0	1	0	(transferred to address C)

FIGURE 1

In most modern computers the input unit takes the form of a console containing keys for starting, stopping, and resetting, a typewriter keyboard for the manual insertion of data, and devices to read instructions and data from punched cards, punched tape, or magnetic tape.

The main memory, consisting of an arrangement of cores such as we have described, is called a rapid access memory. There is also generally an auxiliary or "slow access" memory consisting of magnetic tapes or drums from which data and instructions are brought into the main memory when needed. When data are lodged in a memory address, they replace any information already there. But data taken from storage are copied rather than removed and stay in the address unless erased by a specific instruction.

Output devices take information from the main memory and generally record it on cards, tapes, or printed copy. Some also display it on cathode ray tube units.

The first step towards preparing a set of instructions for the computer is generally to make a diagrammatic scheme of the task to be given it. This is called a "flow chart." Figure 2 is a basic flow chart for a computer operation to assess damage to target forces in a naval war game. However, such charts are still far from telling the computer how to do its job. The next step is to prepare more detailed charts, sometimes called "block diagrams," dealing with the procedure for processing data at intermediate stages. These stages, represented by the rectangular "boxes" in the flow chart, are generally quite complicated and deal with arithmetical processes.

When the sequence of operations has been set out in this way, the charts are used as guides in writing the *program*. To do this in the computer's own coded language, however, would be a highly specialized and time-consuming business. A faster method has been found in the use of "programming languages" such as FORTRAN (Formula Translation Language), COBOL (Common Business Oriented Language), and SIMSCRIPT (Simulation Script), which are not too far removed from everyday language.

A program written in one of these languages is recorded on cards or tapes and fed into the computer together with a "processor." This is another program—in effect a kind of dictionary—that translates the first into coded instructions which the control unit can understand. (When the computer has been equipped in this way, the user at the keyboard may well have the feeling that he is conversing with a human intellect, particularly when he misspells a word and the machine gives a puzzled buzz and prints "Eh?")

Before being able to compute, however, the computer must also be fed with the necessary data and probably with a number of so-called subroutines. These are sets of instructions for performing recurrent processes, such as the finding of square roots, which the main program can simply refer to without having to spell them out each time. Subroutines may also be used to cover sections of the intended operation that may need to be taken out at some time and replaced by alternatives, without the necessity of rewriting the whole program. In computer war games they can be used for the selection of random numbers.

When the start key is pressed, the computer control unit locates the first stored instruction, interprets it, and commands the first operation to be performed. It then takes the next instruction, and so on, until all the data have been processed out or it reaches a halt instruction. In many operations, particularly war games, an instruction near the end will cause the computer to go back to the beginning and repeat what it has done with a different set of data, or an incremental change in one factor—for example, an increase in the speed of an aircraft or the range of a gun. In a nuclear war game variations can be given to the probability of different interception or delivery systems malfunctioning, or the percentage of the population evacuated from cities. By instructing the computer to continue in this way until some final figure is reached, it is possible to cover a wide range of variables. When the operation is complete, or perhaps at intermediate stages in the case of a long operation, the program instructs the computer to "print out." It then turns the

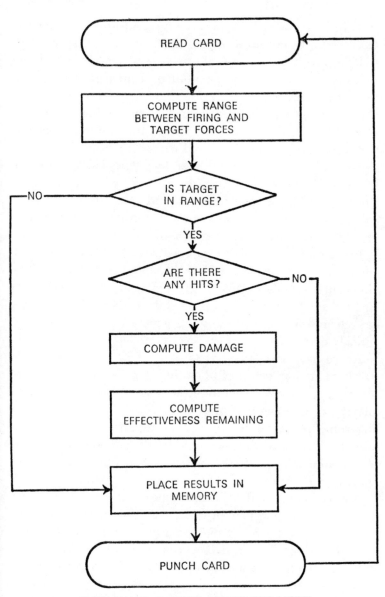

FLOW CHART—DAMAGE ASSESSMENT MODEL

FIGURE 2

facts in its memory back into the original programming language, and the output unit puts them onto a high-speed typewriter capable of printing up to 312,000 characters per minute. A sample of the printout of a nuclear war game is given in Figure 3.

Despite the arithmetically cumbersome method of some of its operations, the computer's ability to complete 1,000,000 arithmetical operations a second makes it extremely fast. On the other hand the compilation of data, flow charts, block diagrams, and a program—plus the "debugging" of the program through checks of each step by hand calculation or a desk calculator—is a lengthy task. It is therefore in the matter of repetition that its timesaving is really felt.

Its second characteristic is accuracy. For although computers are capable of mistakes through electronic malfunction—an example occurred when a computer "forgot" to include 200 helicopters in the 1968 American defense budget —such mistakes are rare and are generally so gross as to be quickly detectable.

As we have seen, there are two ways in which computers are used in war games. Either they can be programmed to simulate the whole operation, acting as both Control and players, or they can perform only part of the operation, leaving some of the decision making to human players. But whether a game is wholly or only partly computerized, or for that matter manual, it is technically a "model"—a term we must now explain.

A model has been described as a means of simulating future conditions under which an event may be expected to occur. In laboratory research it may be a model aircraft in a wind tunnel. In logistical or civilian economic analysis the model may take the form of a chart or graph, which in turn may be represented by an equation or equations, or so-called mathematical model. A model may also be found in the form of a payoff matrix (of which an example may be found on page 170) used to study problems of Game Theory.

	BLUE	RED
Missile Occupancy =	.95	.00
Number of Bombers =	700.00000	435.00000
Warheads per Missile =	1.00000	1.00000
o/o Missile on Missile =	.00000	.20000
o/o Missiles Remaining =	.92443	1.00000
PK Missile on Missile =	.54000	.64000
Missile Targeting Mode =	2.00000	1.00000
WH Missile on Missile =	1.00000	1.00000
Effective PKM on M =	.54000	.64000
o/o Missile on Defense =	.00000	.20000
o/o Missile on Bombers =	.40000	.40000
o/o Missile on Cities =	.60000	.20000
PK Missile on Defense =	.46000	.46000
PK Missile on Bomber =	.45000	.45000
PK Missile on City =	.43000	.45000
Number of Defenses =	109.00000	264.00000
Number of Fields =	64.00000	54.00000
Number of Cities =	500.00000	400.00000
Cities Missile Defended =	50.00000	60.00000
Missile Defense Survival =	.25000	.25000
WH Missile on Defense =	1.00000	1.00000
WH Missile on Field =	5.18519	2.71875
WH Missile on City =	1.00000	1.00000
WH Missile on Def. City =	1.33333	1.00000
Effective PK M on D =	.46000	.46000
Effective PK M on B =	.19579	.29542
Effective PK M on C =	.43000	.45000
Effective PK M on Def. C =	.10568	.1125
Missiles Remaining =	647.10400	435.00000
Cities Destr. (U) by M =	5.62500	7.81542
Cities Destr. (D) by M =	16.65000	135.15229
Number of Bombers =	300.00000	245.00000
Bomber Occupancy =	3.28125	1.95918
Fighter Kill Prob. =	.56000	.55000
Fields Remaining =	12.597693	3.32062
Bombers Remaining =	131.33618	145.71022
o/o Bombers Remaining =	.43779	.59474
Defenses Remaining =	21.12195	255.71637
Fighter KP Remaining =	.10852	.53274
Fighter KP Rem. (Int.) =	.35439	.55000
o/o Bomber on City =	.97097	.84220
o/o Bomber on Defenses =	.02903	.15780
Number Bombs per Bomber =	4.00000	3.00000
PK Bomber on Defenses =	.97000	.96000
PK Bomber on City =	.89000	.89000
WH Kill/Bomber Kill =	.80000	.75000

FIGURE 3

The most complex models are those which are nearest to reality, which is not to say that the simpler ones are easier to construct. For instance, two Marine Corps colonels fighting a war game over Cuba are a much subtler model of a real campaign than a computer trying to do the same thing. (An exercise with troops, involving the transmission of orders through a chain of subordinates, would be more complex still.) This is because the human brain can still perform a much wider variety of processes than the most elaborate electronic computer. A computer can handle much more *data;* but it cannot make qualitative judgments or, except in the crudest way, which we shall see later on, deal with intangible factors such as leadership and morale. Even in the physical and measurable sphere, there is a constant necessity to simplify models before computers can handle them.

A model of the kind that computers in defense establishments handle every day would be a war game to ascertain the best design for a tank. On the assumption that for some limiting reason, say the automotive power available, the speed, firepower, and armor-thickness of a tank are interrelated and that one cannot be increased without decreasing the others, the game might take the form of a series of simulated tank duels in which different pairs of factors are varied in turn. The results of one set of engagements might be used to construct a graph showing the point at which the protection afforded by additional armor is offset by the slow speed of maneuver. Another set could examine the effect of trading off armor for a heavier gun, until a point was reached at which the greater range and penetration of the gun was offset by vulnerability. A third set could explore the effect of sacrificing firepower to mobility. Finally a game might be set up to examine the effect of varying armor-thickness, firepower, and speed in combination. This would be quite a complicated game. But in fact there would be other variable factors affecting the outcome of any tank engagement: the amount of ammunition that could be carried in each tank, the size of the silhouette it presented to the enemy, and so on. At some point, if the game were not to become too complicated, some variables would have to be excluded from consideration.

A common method of doing this is to make a "sensitivity test." In the tank game one sensitivity test could take the form of a preliminary game to assess the number of rounds fired in tank engagements of varying duration and character. It might then be found that beyond a certain point, well within the capacity of any possible design, the number of rounds carried per tank was not of critical importance, and the ammunition factor could be excluded. Of course, in an actual battle there could be many other critical factors, such as the position of the sun and the length of time the tank crews had been without sleep. But although such factors might be considered in an *operational* war game, they would not be relevant to questions of tank design.

We have so far been speaking of combat simulation by general purpose computers, which are most commonly used in war gaming. But a higher degree of realism and complexity may be possible when special purpose computers are used. These may be either digital or of the analog type [2] and are frequently built into a complete simulation system.

The most perfect war game using special purpose computers is probably the automatic flight simulator used for training pilots. Though "war game" may seem an odd description for this apparatus, the point may become clearer if we regard the simulator as the mechanical representation of

[2] The essential difference between digital and analog computers is the way in which variables are represented inside them. In an analog computer there is a continuously varying physical quantity corresponding to the continuous variation of the variable which is represented. A slide rule is a nonelectronic form of analog computer. In a digital computer, when a variable changes by more than a certain amount, its representation jumps discontinuously to a new value. Ordinary computer war games mostly use digital computers—the type we have described. For a full explanation of the differences between the two types see Hollingdale and Tootill, *op. cit.*

a contest between the pilot and his environment. In the modern simulator, the pilot and copilot, sitting in an elaborate replica of the flight deck or cockpit, have all the controls of an actual aircraft. The manipulation of any one of them leads to the reproduction of effects, including climbing and banking attitudes, instrument readings, and even engine noise, which would be caused in "real life." These effects are not directly mechanical, but are the product of many factors —airspeed, crosswinds, altitude, load distribution, etc.—simulated by analog computers. Another function of the computers is to work out the "aircraft's" flight path and indicate, for example, its point of lift-off or touch-down on the imaginary airport runway.

Viewed as a game, the interest of the whole operation lies in its close approximation to reality. The computers operate in "real time," i.e., neither faster nor slower than the real life happenings they simulate. There are no arbitrary assumptions built into the system, since everything in the operation of an aircraft is known and open to accurate representation. Nor is this altered by the fact that an instructor can cause the computer to simulate an in-flight malfunction, such as engine failure, to test the pilot's reactions.

In 1967, after much research, a tactical simulation system almost as close to reality as the flight simulator was developed for the U.S. Air Force by the Raytheon electronics company and set up at Eglin Air Force Base, Florida. Known as AFWET (Air Force Weapons Effectiveness Testing) the "game" is played in a cylindrical volume of air space 100 nautical miles in diameter and 70,000 feet high. It simulates combat involving anything from two to twenty-six units—aircraft, antiaircraft weapons or ground units—of which up to sixteen can be mobile and ten static. The main feature is that actual aircraft are used, and that every movement, including the flight of the aircraft and the firing of each shell or rocket, is monitored by telemetry devices. The only difference from live combat is that the weapons themselves do not "go." Instead, the firing information is fed via the telemetry stations to computers on the ground. The IBM computers then calculate in "real time" the effect of the fire, saying "kill" or "no-kill," according to the parts of the target "hit." The results are simultaneously projected on an information device for the use of the directing staff, and recorded on tape for later evaluation of the effectiveness of weapons or tactics.

AFWET approximates closely to war, not only in its use of human material, but also because tactical movements are executed on the orders of Red and Blue commanders and not at the whim of individual pilots. It also makes very few "assumptions." (The chief is that the computer's "kill" verdict is determined to some extent probabilistically on the basis of laboratory tests of the weapons and targets involved.) But this very realism makes AFWET unique among mechanized war games. We shall find that there are very many questionable assumptions, and simplifications of real world complexity, when we turn to *fully* computerized games— particularly those which claim to be able to tell us the outcome of a thermonuclear war.

7

THE WAR GAMERS

IN A FULL COMPUTER war game every step must be preconceived by the game designers. If an unexpected contingency arises, an umpire cannot step in to solve it, or hold up the game until a new rule is made. The only way to change the logic of the program is to rewrite the routine. For this reason the preparation of a computer game usually begins with the construction of a manual one. In this the designers examine all the events that are liable to occur in the model and the interactions between them. Only when this has been done, and the sequences of military operations clearly established, can a start be made to translate the model into flow charts and block diagrams. In the case of a large-scale game this work of preparation, including the writing, testing, and debugging of the program, may take months or even years.

Another aspect of computer games is that since their input must be described numerically, qualitative factors such as courage and military skill must either be disregarded or, if included, given some quite crude type of representation. Consequently computer games are more often used to represent air or sea war, with their higher degree of mechanization, than land war with its untidy human complications—though (see Chapter 9) this has not discouraged the true enthusiasts.

One basic decision which must be taken early on by the designers of a computer game model is whether it is to be a "deterministic" game or one of the so-called Monte Carlo type. In deterministic models the outcome of events is determined by "expected values." For example, the probability of a bomber penetrating enemy defenses in a given situation might be given a value of 0.20, and the probability of its then destroying a given type of target a value of 0.50. A deterministic game in which 100 sorties were represented would thus end up by showing exactly 10 targets destroyed.

In the Monte Carlo type of game the results are decided by the use of a random process such as we saw in the Marine Corps Landing Force War Game. In a computer game this is generally done by feeding the computer with sheaves of random numbers, for selection in sequence, before the game starts. Such numbers can be bought ready-made from the Rand Corporation in a thick book costing $15. If the Monte Carlo method were used in our bomber game, one play might produce an outcome of seven targets destroyed, another an outcome of fifteen, another an outcome of 0, and so on. (Though, in accordance with the law of probability, the more plays there were, the closer the average would work out to ten.)

The advantage of the Monte Carlo method, which obviously increases the work of analyzing results, is that it presents the analysts with a *distribution* of possible outcomes. This might seem to make it more reliable and "scientific," and, in a sense, it is. But it is important to remember that neither type of game can ever be more valid than the assumptions which go into estimating the various probabilities in the first place.

As the reader may recall from the Introduction (page ix), between 1960 and 1963 the U.S. Department of Defense ran a war game called STAGE (Simulation of Total Atomic Global Exchange) whose outcome purported to show that America would "prevail" in any thermonuclear war with the Soviet Union. STAGE took three years to prepare and five months to play; and the running of a single engagement could last thirty hours.

It would be helpful, in describing a game like STAGE, to be able to reproduce some of the flow charts involved in its construction. But not surprisingly the Pentagon keeps these secret. One must therefore be content with imagining some thousands of pages of logical diagrams representing the war to be simulated both grossly and in detail. The gross representation will include, in logical sequence, such questions as how many bombers (or missiles) are committed by each side, the order of their commitment, each side's choice of targets (of what nature and range), the priority accorded to various targets by the defenses, and so on. There will also be the fundamental question: Which side strikes first, Blue or Red? The detailed representation will have to cover the behavior and interaction of hundreds of individual units such as the bomber whose mission is described by the flow chart in Figure 4. In this the bomber is ordered to take off, refuel in flight, penetrate the enemy's defenses, attack a specified target, and return to a recovery base. A former USAF officer has described the mission thus:

> Does the bomber take off in time? This may be a function of yes–no questions concerning the reliability of communications, security of the bomber's base, whether the bomber is in commission, etc. Does the refueling occur on schedule? Again a series of questions, this time relating to the performance of the tanker aircraft, accuracy of rendezvous, success in coupling, etc. Is the penetration successful? Here we can expect that the series of yes–no questions proceeds from a stochastic [Monte Carlo] process. . . . Probabilities will be

based on assumptions or experience concerning per cent of failure (or success) of the enemy air defenses against bomber penetrations. Does the bomber find its target? Again a series of yes–no questions, attuned perhaps to radar failure, navigational error, weather conditions, etc. Are "bombs away" at the correct bomb release line? Another series of yes–no questions. Does the aircraft return successfully . . . ?[1]

Not every nuclear or air war game involves the computation of every unit's performance. What generally happens is that one part of the action is worked out in detail and the results applied, with various "safeguards," to other events at that level. Even so, the whole operation can remain enormously complex—particularly when basic choices of political or military strategy have to be "ground in" by restraints on the use of certain weapons or bases.

However, except from the narrowest technical point of view, the chief interest of computer games lies not in their mechanics but in the assumptions which go into them—and these often worry the war gamers themselves.

At first sight nuclear rocket warfare might indeed seem highly automated. But leaving aside obvious human aspects such as the suffering, disease, and moral collapse that would result from a nuclear war, the human element involved in actually waging it would be considerable. This element, which the computer has difficulty in handling, resides in the chain of command-and-control, despite efforts to replace it by electronic control mechanisms.

At the lower end of the chain there are the officers commanding missile batteries and Polaris submarines. It is they who must press buttons and turn master keys before a nuclear missile can be launched. When the first intercontinental missiles were installed on American launching sites, each missile control console was manned by two officers, holding separate keys. Each had to turn his key simultaneously in

[1] S. F. Giffin, *The Crisis Game* (New York: Doubleday and Co., 1965).

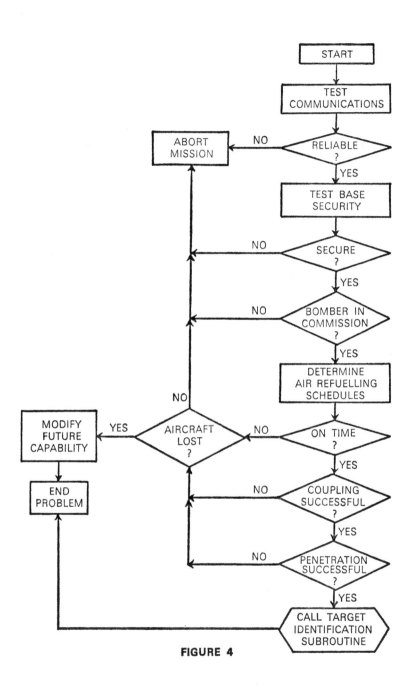

FIGURE 4

widely separated locks before the missile could be armed on receipt of orders from Washington. This "fail-safe" procedure, to prevent an unauthorized launching by one madman, has been superseded by an electronic device called the Permissive Action Link, cosily abbreviated to PAL. But PAL cannot launch a missile; it can only permit it to be launched. The launching must still be performed by officers.

In due course it may be found possible to eliminate the use of officers at the lowest level, and control a large number of missiles from a central point. The commander of a Minuteman complex already has eight to ten missiles under his direct operational control. But even if the human element is reduced to a minimum, except for maintainenance (or, in submarines, navigational purposes), there will still be at least one man in the system—the President. And he will remain the most human actor of all, because, more than the well-drilled missile officer cut off from the world in his submarine or underground control capsule, he will be intimately aware of what will happen when he presses the button.

To put it in these terms is already to oversimplify the situation, however. For the decision the President would face would not be whether to press a button launching America's whole missile force in response to an all-out attack. It would rather be *which* button to press—launching how many missiles, and at what targets—in reply to a *limited* attack. And he would be conscious that if he chose wrongly, the situation would pass beyond his control.

Obviously a computer war game cannot predict what a President would do in this situation. It can only show the results to be expected from this or that decision, adjusted to delays of, say, 5, 10, 15, or 20 minutes before taking it. (A delay of 20 minutes, the maximum warning time for a missile attack, could mean that part of America's retaliatory force no longer existed.) These results, expressed in terms of cities destroyed, missiles remaining, etc., may have some mathematical validity in relation to the scenario, e.g., that the enemy struck with such-and-such forces. But the overall picture presented will be no more reliable than the inspired guesses at Russian or American reactions which the designers put into the game program. In other words, a computer war game merely takes uncertainties out of the actual play and puts them into the assumptions made in its construction.

Sometimes this unreality is avoided by making the game a man-machine game. In this case "Presidential" decisions may be taken by a human player, whose fallibility as an actor is more obvious. But there are still assumptions in a strategic nuclear game which many experienced officers question. These include assumptions about the performance of the military equipment involved.

For example, a ballistic missile may fail in its mission in three ways: by a failure to "go" at launching, by failing to penetrate enemy defenses, or by a failure to reach its target through an early guidance error. Since it is very expensive to launch missiles for test purposes, tests of operational missiles are made largely by connecting electronic monitors to missiles in their launching silos. This yields figures for the expected number of malfunctions. But Air Force critics are factually correct when they point out that it is no equivalent of the fitness statistics of manned aircraft flying regular peacetime training missions.

There is considerable disagreement among defense analysts themselves about the use that can be made of computer games, at least outside the most basic kind of weapons analysis. The doubters become increasingly uneasy the closer they are to discussing situations of the "once only" type, such as an all-out nuclear war, to which the law of probability is irrelevant.

In 1967 I discussed the question with a number of experts of the Rand Corporation.

The most down-to-earth view was expressed by a scientist called Rheinhard, who had seen active service in World War

I. Quantitative analysis, he said, might be a reasonable guide in the study of systems, but not for the study of particular possibilities. You couldn't game Lee at Second Bull Run without relying on the most absurd kind of number check. When you came to gaming the unknown, i.e., nuclear war, you had to make the grossest assumptions. "The first mushroom cloud, and the enemy—or, God help us, our own troops —may run like hell." Of course, you can assume that good training will ensure firmness. Or you can say that when a certain number of casualties occur, the line will break. But who knows?

A more tolerant, but nevertheless qualified, view was taken by another Rand expert, M. G. Weiner.

"A game," said Weiner, across a table littered with computer printout, "is a *simple* model of the world. But to start gaming, you have to have a simple model. Basically it is a confrontation between two symbolically represented military forces. What kind of confrontation do you want? Political? Military? Why are they in this confrontation? What options would they have in this situation? This is the kind of question you have to ask. But by using a simplified model you're dealing in delimited options.

"You could say you're interested only in options which are of interest to your clients. But this would be unfair to your clients. Or you could delimit the options by time, for example by using random number generation to decide which ones you're going to examine. But this is also unsatisfactory. In fact any answer is bound to be unsatisfactory, because of the physical limitations you face.

"Of course, you could say that the trouble with computers is that you just shift the problem to another locus. How much confidence do you have in the rules you have now written? But they have their advantages. For example, in a manual game on limited war (that represents about 50 percent of the activity I'm engaged in) the questions might be: How much restraint is to be placed on certain targets? Are nuclears to be allowed, or not allowed? Are you allowed to overfly certain friendly countries or not? Each of these questions would require a separate game. But the computer will include a capability for these uncertainties. So in this way you can see different ways of using your forces."

I asked Weiner what, in "limited war," were the aims of war gaming.

He said they were multiple. They might be used to decide the right mix of, say, aircraft to buy, in which case you ran a series of games based on various mixes to decide how many aircraft you wanted of each kind. Or they could be used to determine the requirements in a certain situation: for example, if the United States or its allies were involved, what personnel and logistic support would be needed. Or they could be used to examine concepts, for example the concept of military assistance. What might be the result if, instead of giving allies more hardware, you provided them with infrastructure that would help their domestic economy?

He mentioned a game series which had been run, some years before, on war in Vietnam. Each game had assumed three levels of conflict: war that was "little more than internal revolution," "low-level" war, and "high-level" war (in which Russia and China both joined). Economic and political scientists had dealt with the political and economic outcomes; the final report had dealt with *all* the outcomes. The military result was that in low-level war the investment in infrastructure paid better, because national forces could be moved more rapidly. The prime purpose of this, as of other game series, had been to expose problems and issues, "to achieve attitudinal impact rather than measurable results."

Weiner said that war game solutions tended to be seized upon if they accorded with a would-be policy maker's intuitions. But since by definition they dealt with military choices, they intruded on the role of military officers and provoked resistance. The military felt that their intuitive judgments could never be made explicit. "It all depends on the situation at the time," was the soldier's stock answer to questions of contingency. But the analyst *could* make judgments explicit, by showing the alternatives and why they had been discarded.

Another Rand expert with definite views on computer games was Frederick Sallagar, a senior staff member of the Social Science Division.

Sallagar said he was mainly interested in the interaction between civil and military events ("as anyone must be who is interested in anything less than cataclysmic war"). He was not against computer games for dealing with mathematical factors, e.g., the effects of a nuclear strike, but there were three serious objections to their use for any other purpose. "To begin with, the only reason for the trouble of setting up computer models is to manipulate variables. But these are valid only if you are interested in the more trivial values, and the effect of these on the broader problems is always small.

"Of course," he added, "it's different if you're interested in specifications of different types of aircraft and so on. But again, this assumes that war games are the proper context in which to test these variables, especially if you are thinking years ahead of a war against an undefined enemy.

"Secondly, to set up a computer model, which has a necessarily limited number of variables, you have to aggregate; and you may aggregate out the most important ones. Thirdly, it's difficult to introduce political variables, which can't be represented by numbers. So you have to make a set of assumptions about political factors at the start of the game and hold these static.

"Fourthly, many outcomes and results of war games are completely determined by the assumptions which go into them. It's very difficult, even for an honest researcher, to keep this completely clear. Not only the maker of the model, but everyone down to the programmer, must make assumptions. They may be aware of the assumptions in their own field;

but then they may not be aware of the *significance* of these assumptions. They may not be able to make clear to the reader the assumptions which may have affected the result."

Sallagar said that the objections to computer games applied particularly in the case of broader research, including the testing of force structures and systems. For this reason he had developed a different kind of game whose object was to have military action take place in a valid political context, and to "replace prophecy about the future with something more useful."

"It's military practice," he explained, "to speak of the 'most likely' time and locale of a conflict. But this leads to the wrong criteria for research purposes. If you want to study nuclear weapons in a game, you have to bring about a war situation in which they would be used. You've got to ask: Does this situation preclude nuclears? If it does, you must change the scenario. Now, most war games put credibility first, and relevance to the research situation second. My contribution has been to reverse this. I don't think you can speak of relative credibility. For example, the Pearl Harbor attack was ruled out as incredible, and General Ridgway was almost court-martialed for suggesting it. The Cuban missiles were also ruled out as too 'incredible' for a game situation." I gathered that two of Sallagar's games had been played at Rand, one taking a year and the other six months, but that they had been called off for want of manpower.

I asked Sallagar whether he thought all the effort put into war games in America had achieved anything.

He said that back in the days of the Eisenhower administration, "when limited war was not a very popular concept," they had been valuable in showing how, under certain conditions, limited war could involve two major powers and even the use of nuclear weapons. They had shown the military, who were obsessed with massive retaliation strategy, how such a war could come about through one side or the other mistaking the effect of its actions. "It *could* have happened," he added—though lessons had since been learned from Cuba. I asked if he didn't think Schelling's development of communications theory had helped show ways of avoiding the danger. But he said: "Schelling goes too far; he's one of the chess players." The "chess players," he explained, were people—mostly without government experience—who assumed that decision makers always acted rationally in full possession of the facts. This wasn't the case, and to prove it he cited the example of the escalation of the air war between Britain and Germany in World War II. "Escalation," said Sallagar, "is often just a *bureaucratic* step."

Not to my surprise, I received somewhat more confident answers when I talked about computer games with those committed to the use of them at official Defense establishments, though even here there were more reservations than I expected. At the Army's Strategy and Tactics Analysis Group (STAG) I was told a model was under development that would show under what circumstances escalation would take place in a military confrontation irrespective of the intentions of either side. I was also told of the development of a model intended to identify the role of the "chicken factors." [2] One analyst said that *all* manual games would be superseded by computer models as methods were found for representing factors that were now regarded as "unquantifiable." Another said he could think of at least ten major improvements brought about in the United States defense posture as a result of computer gaming—"force mixes, types of force bought, forces in being, that sort of thing." The dollar savings had been "almost dramatic," he added.

The kind of game that STAG played seemed fairly high-powered. A sample game problem was "Can the Soviets now have 1,000 intercontinental rockets?" The answer to this, I was told, could be obtained without Intelligence by analyzing Soviet construction programs in other fields and measuring

2 The strategic game of "chicken" is described in Chapter 10.

these against Russia's industrial resources. "But, of course," someone said, "there *are* assumptions in this kind of game. When the game's over and you turn in your analysis, you write page after page saying 'Please remember this is all based on certain assumptions'—but there'll always be somebody who forgets all the same."

There was a story at STAG about one of these games to determine Soviet war capacity. The parameters included specified numbers of air wings, divisions, and naval units, and one of the tasks was to assess the amount of food, fuel, mechanical spares, etc., that would be needed to support an invasion of Western Europe. The game started manually but was overtaken by mechanization. To feed the computer it was necessary to know things like the "average" weight of a truck battery. "I remember trying to work it out from a Sears Roebuck catalogue," said one of the game staff. "Another question was: If a truck got knocked out on the battlefield, how long did it take, on the average, to repair it? But what was an 'average' battlefield? How long did it take to reach the 'average' repair depot? The answers just weren't obtainable in a way that made sense."

"But along the line," I was told, "some insights fell out. We did [statistical] tests that nobody expected to be workable." One thing revealed was that a prolonged war in Europe would come to a halt at the end of a year for want of penicillin production.

The main work at STAG was described to me as being the analysis of organizational and weapons requirements and the testing of concepts: for example, should one spend X billion dollars on Nike-X (the Army's antimissile system) or on some other antimissile system, or should one forego an antimissile system altogether and spend the money on offensive missiles instead? And what type of control should there be in a system —should there be highly sophisticated guidance and fewer weapons, or less complicated guidance and more weapons? If the system was of interservice interest, STAG's job was to come up with the Army's requirements after consulting the other services about theirs.

Similarly wide-ranging studies engage the computers of the Navy, whose war-gaming "library" includes two separate models for strategic war, NEMO (Nuclear Exchange Model) and COBRA (Computer Blast and Radiation Assessment). NEMO can simulate nuclear war with thirty-one different types of missile and 3,000 launchers on each side in less than an hour and tell you by how much each missile missed its target. COBRA picks up the pieces, as it were, and tells you the damage done and what forces you still have left.

The rest of the Navy's fifteen computer game models are mainly for antisubmarine and air war. A complicated antisubmarine game may take thirty minutes to run through the computer; some air war games take three. But it takes up to two years to write up the war plan for a major game, and six months to write up the results.

The Navy uses computer games as readily as the other services, but is decently reserved about the findings. "Garbage in equals garbage out," said one officer cheerfully, adding that in a good proportion of "runs" weapons performance was deliberately downgraded "because there's always some hardnosed son of a gun in the fleet who says he finds his equipment falls short of the manufacturer's claims."

There were other Navy war games which somehow never surfaced during my conversations with naval analysts, though their names came up in other places. There was a pair of games called Great Circle I and Great Circle II which appeared to concern the Polaris program; and a game in 1963 which had shown that the aircraft carrier had a long and glorious future. And somewhere in Washington was a game to which all three services had contributed information, to provide a basis of the nuclear war "dead figures" regularly presented to Congress in the early 1960s.

But the biggest user of computer games is the Air Force. I asked an Air Force analyst what kind of games these were, and he said: "The games at the upper end of the spectrum are built on all-out nuclear holocausts on both sides; at the other end we're down to a very limited tactical war where you're using three ground divisions in some area with a few fighter aircraft for support. And in the area in between—the area in the iron bomb or preventive type of war if you will —you have anything from one or two divisions deployed in an underdeveloped area to about twenty divisions in a highly developed area." Our dialogue proceeded:

Q: How much do you game on computers?

A: The total nuclear exchange is very easy to computerize. We can, and generally do, use computers.

Q: Then your game model is purely military; it doesn't allow for political circumstances such as the indecision of a President?

A: Well, the politico-military type of game is done at the Joint War Games agency. We always assume that the decision to respond *is* made. What we *can* do, in our games, is to introduce time lags; for example between the moment Red launches his weapons and the moment that the chief decision maker gives the order to respond, and between this decision and the actual retaliation. The thing is to examine the effects of delaying decisions. At what time do we react to the threat? We may preempt, for example, knowing that he's going to attack. What are the effects? What are the effects if we make the decision five minutes after he's launched? What are the effects if we make it five minutes after first impact?

Q: But when you come to "limited war," and a lot of factors can't be quantified, do you still use computer games?

A: We can still use computers to a limited extent, but we use them like a fast adding machine. Given your forces and your dispositions, you can sit down and compute losses. Nevertheless, you can't computerize the whole scene because there are so many decisions that the players themselves have to make—about locations, say. The player can say: "I'm going to employ this or that number of bombers against some array of the enemy's airfields." But then he has to decide: What percent of them am I going to put against these airfields, what percent against his front line elements, what percent against his radar installations on a particular day. Well, it all depends on the situation you're facing on that particular day, so of course these decisions can't really be preplanned. And they can't be put into a computer; the computer doesn't know what decisions to make.

Q: How long do your Air Force games take?

A: Normally four to eight months may elapse before your first run of a computer game. And again, depending on what you're looking for, you're not going to make just one run. You're going to make a series and compare the analyses. To do that might take a couple of months. So you could say you take anywhere from six months to a year. In a limited war or combat game you may feel you have to play day by day, for perhaps a thirty-day war. If you're playing a really elaborate game of this type manually, you can't hope to finish it before a year. But of course, you're never satisfied; you always want to know more. But life in the Pentagon being what it is, the moment comes when you have to say "Well, what have I learned?" When a series of games runs for more than a year, you begin to feel nervous. So we seldom set target dates for more than a year. When the year's up, if we have indeed produced some interesting game, and it's decided we want to learn something more, then we continue on.

Q: Who provides the players for your games, the analysis section or other branches of the Air Force?

A: There was a time when we were a small group, about a hundred people I think, when we still didn't have all the expertise that we should have. So for a tactical game we might ask for people from, say, Tac HQ. They would be sent on detachment for a number of months. But the headquarters complained that they couldn't keep sending people down and still carry on with their own day-to-day business. Now we have a permanent group of officers who stay for three or four years. Every year newcomers come in and they bring experience from the field. That's what makes this kind of organization tick. Sure, we've got analysts: some very good ones. But unless you have real life blood for analysis it becomes a sort of stagnant exercise.

Q: I gather that all your games are "open"; each side knows what the other is planning. But does this give a valid picture?

A: It helps explore a kind of game theory. If I use Strategy One, does it force the enemy to use Strategy Two? It helps probe weakness. Suppose, say, the enemy's highly dependent on his radars for vectoring his fighter aircraft against my incoming bombers. If I go for these radars, how far have I degraded his effectiveness against me? Can I now say that I don't have to go after his antiaircraft guns?

This is the kind of strategy that's played and examined.

Q: How do the lessons get passed out to the Air Force?

A: Usually the Chiefs of Staff say "This is significant; go out and brief all the units on this one." First the units will look at it pretty skeptically, because it comes from the Pentagon. Then they'll try to get at it in every possible way they can. Is it right or wrong? Now once it's decided "Yes, it's a good maneuver," it becomes part of the policy of the service. It doesn't go directly from our analysis into the training schools.

Q: How do you see the payoff from war gaming?

A: It's difficult to say. I don't think we ever really know the extent to which our analysis influences doctrine. I think policy makers could make policy without the benefit of analysis, and the policy might be good. We don't really know if it's good or not until we put it to the ultimate test. All we can really do is give these policy makers a firmer base on which to base decisions. To what extent do we influence these decisions? They have to make these decisions anyway, without analysis. The fact that we give them additional insight into the ramifications of making this decision or that decision has probably been helpful to them. But to say there has been any influence on any particular finding is difficult, because it's involved with many things that impinge on the decision— types of forces they'd like to have, types that they can have from a budgetary point of view, and so on. We know that war games *do* have influence; but the extent to which this influence has dominance over others—I don't know.

8

THE SYSTEMS
ANALYSIS DEBATE

IN THE PENTAGON ARCHIVES is a film of a strategic air war game whose scenario involves a nuclear exchange between Russia and America. The whole thing exists on tens of thousands of computer punch cards. As Soviet warheads hit American targets, B-52s of Strategic Air Command, on permanent airborne alert, start moving towards Russia. They rendezvous with aerial tankers, change course to deceive Soviet defenses, activate electronic countermeasures, lose a good part of their number to surface-to-air missiles, and succeed in obliterating Moscow in return for New York. As they turn to "de-penetrate" the Soviet defenses, information is received that their recovery base in Britain no longer exists. One of the many purposes of the game, as I recall, is to discover feasible alternatives in Spain and Iceland.

I asked an Air Force operational analyst how he could be sure that the vital operational data on which such a game was based were correct. He said that of course war gamers themselves had no means of going out and testing weapons. That had to be left to the organizations which dealt with weapons testing. "We know that these tests are carried out under controlled conditions," he said. "And we know that these conditions will influence the outcome. We also think we know, given information from the test center, what these effects are likely to be. But we can never *really* know."

I pressed him for an opinion on the accuracy of data on *human* performance, and asked whether erroneous data might not produce false results.

"The thing that troubles us," he said with surprising candor, "is that we don't even *know* if our results are erroneous. We may think they're good. We try to evaluate everything that can affect them. But the human factor is something we don't have a handle to. All we can do is to treat people as they act on wartime maneuvers. In some cases we know we're *under*estimating capability, because sometimes there's a new incentive that comes from being in combat. On the other hand sometimes the opposite happens. All we can hope is that on balance it works out in action as it works out on exercises."

Now, as we observed earlier, air war games, particularly "strategic" ones involving nuclear exchanges, are more readily computerized than games which simulate land operations with their many untidy human factors. But in Air Force circles I found a considerable embarrassment in discussing them—not because of the high security classification on matters concerning the nuclear deterrent, but because of deep differences of opinion in the Air Force itself. On one hand there were the missile age technicians, such as the analyst just mentioned, who expressed awareness of the limitations of computer war gaming but were convinced that it made a significant contribution to the selection of systems and strategies. On the other hand there were the "fliers" who, while not ruling out the value of games for instructional purposes, believed that their increasing use in systems analysis had usurped the place of judgment and experience and led the top planners to forget vital military intangibles such as "guts."

The archetype of the latter, now in retirement, is the legendary chief and an architect of SAC, General Curtis LeMay. In 1964, at the height of his battle with the Defense Secretary, Mr. McNamara, over the future of the manned bomber, LeMay reminded a Congressional committee how in World War II, when he had started by commanding a B-17 bomber group in Europe, the theorists had predicted that enemy antiaircraft guns were going to shoot down every bomber that came over. But in fact, he told the committee, "without paying any attention to the [German] defenses we had a loss ratio of less than two percent."

Overlooking the equally false predictions of early air war theorists such as Giulio Douhet and Billy Mitchell that wars of the future would be won by airpower alone, LeMay repeated this story when I visited him in retirement in California in 1967. He also told me another, to show (he said) that war-game results—on which McNamara had partly based his decision to refuse the Air Force the new B-70—were no better than the assumptions that went into them.

"At the end of the war," said LeMay, "I was appointed by General Arnold to take over Air Force Research and Development. We were a long way behind in the analysis business. So we had to catch up. We tried to set up a war-gaming method, and used wartime experience to check it out. At the Aberdeen Proving Ground in Maryland we set up a battle game between B-17s and B-24s on one side and Messerschmitt 109s and 190s on the other. Well, we ran this game out, and the answer it gave us was that the B-17 couldn't live in its environment. There was also another war game, which we set up at Rand. The idea in this game was to see if the German defenses round Berlin had been any good. Well, what this one showed was that the German defenses had been so good that our bombers hadn't even been able to get through."

Everybody, LeMay said, was trying to find a war-gaming method that would answer the question: Do you have a defense or don't you? It was an admirable goal, but it couldn't be reached because you could never be sure of half the factors you put into running it. Take the human factor. With manned systems this was paramount. But even with unmanned systems, i.e., ballistic missile forces, it could be critical. The period of human judgment was short, but it was there nonetheless. Somebody had to push the button. But when? Where? Under what circumstances? Suppose, said LeMay darkly, he didn't push the button at all?

He said airpower was simply a tool in the hands of *people*. It was the people who would fight. "In the atomic business we talk ourselves into a state of shock." Some pinko-type scientists said nuclear war was going to destroy us. But they'd said that about the test program too. It was nonsense. First, if America exploded a device in some situation, it wouldn't necessarily mean an all-out nuclear exchange. Secondly, if there were a nuclear war, it would only be like going back to what he called "the old type of war."

"A lot of people may be killed," he said. "We may have many cities obliterated in the future. But there will be no difference between a city that suffers nuclear attack and the fate of ancient Carthage. Maybe there may be a dozen to fifty Carthages, but there will be no difference so far as the individuals are concerned."

Of course, said LeMay, he didn't want a nuclear war; he didn't want *any* war. "But you don't have to roll over and play dead just because somebody challenges you."

LeMay said that some of the assumptions which went into war games on the reliability of missile performance were extremely doubtful. With airplanes it was different. "When I commanded SAC," he said, "we flew thousands of sorties under the most realistic conditions we could devise. We had extensive records of radars going out, engines going out, bombing error, and so on." But missiles were too expensive to throw away on tests. There were all kinds of ways in which a Polaris or a Minuteman could malfunction, both on the ground and on its way to the target. With regard to launches, you could do any number of drills and checkouts—so long as you stopped short of actually pressing the firing key. Beyond that point—what? It was true, using dummy warheads, you could do a *limited* number of tests over ocean ranges. But what you couldn't do, even if you could afford it, under the Test Ban Treaty, was to test the complete system.

"As far as I know," he added significantly, "only one complete system has ever been fired, and that's Minuteman."

Another redoubtable critic of reliance on computer solutions has been Vice Admiral Rickover, the architect of nuclear propulsion in the U.S. Navy. In May 1966 Rickover told a subcommittee of the House Committee on Appropriations that many people were mesmerized into believing that a study based on computer calculations must be correct since it used the most modern mathematical techniques. They were led, he said, to believe that the results were equivalent to scientific proof. But this was "just not so."

Recalling that his nuclear propulsion work employed "the most advanced computers in the world and . . . a large number of first rank mathematicians, scientists, and engineers," Rickover told the subcommittee.

> . . . hardly a day goes by without experience in our test programs and operating plants revealing that the results of many of our computer studies are not correct; had we based our engineering decisions solely on the computer study results, our nuclear power plants would not work. In my opinion, the ability of the social scientists to calculate numerical values for military effectiveness is even less than our ability to calculate a numerical basis for many of the engineering

decisions we are forced to base on judgment, experience, and intuition. To make the correct engineering decisions requires extensive knowledge and experience in engineering. Mathematical ability alone will not suffice.[1]

Rickover's main target was cost-effectiveness studies in the Department of Defense—a matter in which he had an ax to grind since they had been used by Mr. McNamara to veto the building of a new nuclear-powered carrier, the *John F. Kennedy,* for which he claimed a military value far outweighing its high construction cost. He accused the analysts of being obsessed with cost at the expense of the "effectiveness" side of the cost-effectiveness equation.

"All factors of military effectiveness for which the analyst cannot calculate a numerical value have been automatically discarded from consideration," he said; and went on to point out, with some support from contemporary American experience, that

> . . . all wars and military development should have taught us that . . . a war, small or large, does not follow a prescribed "scenario" laid out in advance. If we could predict the sequence of events more accurately, we could probably avoid war in the first place. The elder Moltke said, "No plan survives contact with the enemy." Are we not learning that bitter lesson every day in Vietnam, just as we have learned it in every other war since the beginning of man?

On the basis of cost-effectiveness, Rickover concluded, the American colonists would not have revolted against George III; the Greeks would not have stood up to the Persians at Marathon; and the British would have made terms with Hitler in 1940.

As presented by Rickover and LeMay, the military case against the computer is twofold: It provides a false basis for

---

[1] Congressional Record. Testimony May 11, 1966, hearings "Department of Defense Appropriations for 1967," Subcommittee on Department of Defense, House Committee on Appropriations, 89th Congress, 2d Session, part 6.

deciding the allocation of defense resources, and it fosters the illusion that one possesses a "scientific" defense. But what if the computer had not been introduced into American military planning? Another side to this question was put in 1966 by Charles Hitch—the man who, under Mr. McNamara, was principally responsible for the introduction into the Department of Defense of the modern defense planning system which goes by the title PPB (planning-programming-budgeting). In a Nuffield Lecture of the Royal Society in London, Hitch described the condition in which he found the Department on his appointment as Assistant Secretary (Comptroller) five years before.

There had been, he said, a total "disarray" because of the almost complete separation between military planning and fiscal planning. Military planning was done by the Joint Chiefs of Staff, fiscal planning by the civilian Comptroller's staff. Each was couched in different terms: the military in terms of army divisions, naval vessels, aircraft squadrons, and so on; the fiscal in terms of budget categories such as personnel, procurement, and research and development. The military plans were either not costed in terms of their budget requirements, or this was done so roughly as to be almost unusable. Moreover the two types of planning were for different time periods. Once a year the Joint Chiefs would produce a massive plan called the Joint Strategic Objective Plan with force estimates projected five to ten years into the future. The Secretary of Defense would file and note it. Then in the budget season, in October and November, the real decisions were made by the civilian secretaries, advised in the main by the Comptroller. The Great Plan itself was simply financially unfeasible, a pasting together of the "wish lists" of the four services. "The system in short did not require the military planners to face up to the hard choices that are part of responsible management."

Before Hitch's arrival, the civilian secretary had to do the best he could in preparing his annual budget review, and the method adopted was the "budget ceiling" approach. The President would indicate the general level of the defense budget he thought appropriate to the international situation and his overall economic and fiscal policies; and the Secretary of Defense, by one means or another, would allocate this figure among the three military departments. Each department would in turn prepare its basic budget submission, allocating its ceiling among its own functions, units, and activities. This was inefficient, because

> . . . each service tended to exercise its own priorities, favoring its own unique missions to the detriment of joint missions, striving to lay the groundwork for an increased share of the budget in future years by concentrating on alluring new weapons systems, and protecting the overall size of its force structure. The Air Force, for example, gave overriding priority to strategic retaliatory bombers and missiles, starving as necessary the tactical air units needed to support Army ground operations and the airlift units needed to move limited war forces quickly to far-off trouble spots. The Navy gave overriding priority to its own nuclear attack forces, notably the aircraft carriers, while its antisubmarine warfare capability was relatively neglected and its escort capability atrophied. The Army used its limited resources to preserve the number of its divisions, although this meant that they lacked equipment and supplies to fight effectively for more than a few weeks. Moreover, because attention was focused only on the next fiscal year, the services had every incentive to propose large numbers of new starts, the full cost dimensions of which would only become apparent in subsequent years.[2]

Hitch and McNamara replaced this with an annually renewed Five Year Program in which military and fiscal planning was combined. The program was organized by "outputs" related to national objectives. Its basic elements were "force units"—army divisions, air wings, weapons systems such as

[2] C. Hitch, Royal Society Nuffield Lecture, London, October 25, 1966.

Minuteman, development projects such as Nike-X, and so on. The sum of such elements, representing the total program of the Defense Department, was about 1,000. In the budget review each element was given with its full annual resource and financial costs for the next five years, regardless of the budget category in which the money was appropriated; and the funds required were kept within the limits which the Defense Secretary thought right and feasible. The function of war games and computers was to aid the latter and the Joint Chiefs of Staff in comparing alternative programs. They thus became part of a centrally directed systems analysis procedure which, according to Hitch, was only one form of "program-planning-budgeting." (The other was traditional military planning, by itself or in combination with the systems approach.) Hitch defined systems analysis as

> . . . nothing more than economic analysis applied to the public sector. Economic analysis is concerned with the allocation of resources. Its maxim is: Maximize the value of objectives achieved minus the value of resources used. In business this reduces itself to maximizing profits. In Defense . . . we lack a common valuation for objectives and resources and therefore have to use one of two weaker maxims—maximize our objectives for given resources, or minimize our resources for given objectives. This is what systems analysis attempts to do—assist the decision maker to choose weapons systems and modes of operating them which maximize some military objective or objectives (for example, the number of attacking bombers or missiles shot down) for given resources (for example, budget dollars) available. The function of the program is to cost out the plans to keep them feasible and realistic, to make the planners face up to hard choices. The function of systems analysis is to get dollars into the calculations at an early stage. . . .

According to Hitch, systems analysis played only a partial role in the total planning and decision-making process. It attempted to "inform and sharpen" the judgment of decision makers; it did not itself make decisions.

In operations research it is customary to distinguish between optimizing and predictive models. In this application the two blend into each other. Our aim is to help the decision maker. What help does he need in making a decision—in choosing between alternatives? He needs to know the consequences of his choices—positive consequences, in achieving his objectives, and negative consequences or "costs" in a broad sense. If he has a single measurable objective and is interested in only one kind of cost—say budget cost—it might well be possible to design an optimizing model—a systems analysis which would, in effect, make the decision for him. I have never encountered such a pure case in the real world, although I know of some which approximate to it. In typical cases there are several objectives, some intangible—and several relevant costs. The systems analyst must predict the important consequences . . . in assisting the decision maker to make his own intuitive choice.

From all this one could gain the impression that systems analysis (or cost-effectiveness study) is a powerful device which could lead to folly if too heavily leaned upon but which —thanks to the wisdom and restraint of its users—has in fact freed American military planning of muddle and unrealism. But before weighing Hitch's defense of systems analysis against the arguments of military critics, we should do well to hear another witness who cannot be accused of ax-grinding: Klaus Knorr, Professor of Economics and Director of the Princeton Center of International Studies.

In 1966 Professor Knorr published an article in the *Bulletin of the Atomic Scientists* in which, after giving his view that cost-effectiveness studies were a valuable tool for elucidating choices in military capabilities, he examined the limitations on their usefulness. This, he said, depended

. . . on the completeness with which costs and benefits can be analyzed. I stress particularly costs other than money, for these can be of great variety and, it seems to me, they are easily lost sight of. They may be political, as when a particular choice causes great inconvenience to any ally, or military, as when a choice engenders a sharp decline in the morale of a service.[3]

To the extent that costs and benefits could not be measured accurately, the problems of choice were not open to rigorous economic analysis, said Knorr.

Another limitation on the cost-effectiveness approach arose from imperfect information.

> In the military area, various incalculable uncertainties must be faced often. Costs may be uncertain, technology may be uncertain, the properties of military conflict situations may be uncertain, and the reactions and capabilities of potential enemy nations are apt to be uncertain. The last uncertainty is of particular import; it is imperative that military choices be examined within a framework of interaction. An opponent's responses to our choices may, after all, curtail or altogether nullify the advantage we seek. Nor is it enough to recognize the conflict aspects of the problem. The possibilities of tacit or formal cooperation may be equally significant.

A third potential limitation of the cost-effectiveness approach, according to Knorr, was

> . . . the salience it inevitably attributes to the criterion of purely monetary costs. . . . Should we not consider whether, in societies becoming more affluent, monetary costs, though important, should not be expected to decline in importance relative to other values? For example would the . . . loss of human life in the event of a conflict not gain importance in relation to the monetary sacrifice?

The cost-effectiveness approach should be given no more influence on decisions than it could legitimately claim, said Knorr. The technique might be a scientific technique, but its application was an *art*. Thus, although there might be nothing wrong with cost-effectiveness as a tool, there could

---

[3] K. Knorr, "On the Cost-effectiveness Approach to military research and development," *Bulletin of the Atomic Scientists,* November 1966.

be a great deal wrong with its exploitation if it was not governed by an inventive imagination and good judgment. Cost-effectiveness studies, he thought, had got less than their due attention before Mr. McNamara became Secretary of Defense. But there was evidence to suggest that subsequently they had received too much. He referred to the nuclear carrier controversy. In a long testimony before a Senate committee, Mr. McNamara had come back "again and again" to the difference in money costs, but

> . . . he never explained why the advantages of the nuclear carrier were not worth the difference in these costs. He contented himself with stating flatly that he did not think they were, while citing eagerly and at length some dubious analogies: Why he personally was better off buying a medium-price rather than a high-price automobile; why a farmer, having to transport produce to the market from time to time, might be better off with a cheaper and slower truck than with a speedier and more expensive one. . . . I had the impression that the money-cost difference and the [oversimplified] cost-effectiveness model were foremost in the Secretary's mind, and that the very complicated guesswork on possible demands on aircraft carriers some years hence were not.

A possible antidote to excessive attention to quantifiable factors was the development of effective models for *qualitative* analysis—if there were people with a wide enough range of skills to design them. Meanwhile he thought too much reliance was being placed on economists and other quantitative analysis experts who did not necessarily command expertise on essentially military, political, and psychological problems. "Quantified common sense" (a virtue extolled by Charles Hitch) might in fact prove a vice, giving "short shrift to the analysis of intangibles" and "leading to deficient scenarios."

The greatest risks in cost-effectiveness studies, said Knorr, were in relation to research and development, where

. . . as experience shows abundantly, financial costs are hard to estimate; technological advance is difficult to predict; and the benefits hard to evaluate. After all, research and development outputs will affect military capabilities only after a considerable time lag and—during this time—the relevant military, technological, and military environment may undergo substantial changes that impinge on the value of a weapon system, or of a strategy for which it is designed. Above all the potential enemies may change significantly, in part perhaps as a result of their reaction to our research and development choices. Even the actual use to which evolving weapons will ultimately be put is hard to predict; history provides numerous examples of new weapons finding uses quite different from these which were originally intended.[4]

The outsider might rightly deduce from all this that there is confusion among defense experts themselves as to the role which systems analysis, and war games, can legitimately fulfill. But on closer examination he will find three points that are more or less beyond dispute. First, that some form of analysis is essential if central decision makers are to arbitrate between the competing claims of military specialists. Second, that the central authority, being obliged to impose peacetime limits on military expenditure, will inevitably be attracted to the use of techniques which purport to reassure it that it retains a capability to defeat, or at least deter, its external enemies. Third, that however much central decision makers defer to the importance of sound intuitive judgment in their work, the bureaucratic nature of the modern state provides a built-in temptation to concentrate analysis on money cost and other quantifiable factors.

Now, the architects of the present-day American decision-making machine are not fools. On the contrary, men such as McNamara and Hitch represent some of the ablest intellects produced by their society. They set as much store by the avoidance of self-destructive conflicts as they do by the secu-

4 *Ibid.*

rity of their nation. Might it not be, the outsider could therefore ask, that the techniques they have introduced are merely *imperfect at the present juncture?* That they could be perfected through the attainment of some of the things suggested by Knorr, particularly models for *qualitative* analysis?

This is a pertinent thought, but not a new one. For the quest for qualitative models in military operational research has been going on for some years. Military social scientists (to use their official description) already play computer games which purportedly enable them to manipulate intangibles such as the morale and loyalty of embattled communities, the economic and political health of nations, the growth of technology, and the magnetism of ideologies. Orthodox systems analysts tend to refer to such game models as "games to solve the universe." The reader may judge for himself whether these attempts can lead anywhere when he reads the next pages. But here a word of caution is necessary. It is not the "workability" of such models that is in question. Most of them can be set up as both manual and computer games and produce the same result from a given situation. But this does not mean that the computer game is "valid," except in the narrowest structural sense. The only way to judge the validity of a computer game is by reference to outcome of events in the real world.

9

GAMING THE
UNGAMABLE

ONE OF THE LEADING users of war games in America is the Advanced Research Projects Agency (ARPA), which has been intimately concerned with such advanced technological projects as the antimissile missile, ocean-bed crawling devices, and orbiting satellites to detect clandestine nuclear plants. But ARPA's activities are not confined to hardware technology. In 1964, when planners began to suspect that the Vietnam war was not responding to their predictions, the Agency commissioned a group called Abt Associates, Inc., of Cambridge, Mass., to explore the feasibility of a computer model that simulated some "major aspects of internal revolutionary conflict."

The idea was that if only the problems of counterinsurgency could be described in terms of a small number of variables, in the same way as physical processes, mathematical analysis could soon solve them. The crux of the problem was how to give the variables, which were essentially qualitative in character, a numerical value that could be understood by a computer.

After studying some twenty case histories of insurgency, Abt Associates decided that the principal variables affecting the outcome of a counterinsurgency campaign were "information," "loyalty," and "effective military force." But before trying to construct a computer model they first set out to explore the effect of these variables in a manual game. They set the game in a rural Southeast Asian context, in which the principal actors were insurgents, villagers, and government forces. It took six months to develop and was worked out in a series of fifteen trial "plays" by Abt Associates staff members, scholars from Harvard and M.I.T., and "area experts" from government agencies. The game came to be called the AGILE-COIN (counterinsurgency) game, or, for short, AGILE.

The first play of AGILE took the form of six "villagers" in the same room being visited alternately by government and insurgent players using variously colored playing cards to represent soldiers, food, and offers of harvesters. In order to win, the insurgents had to keep the loyalty of four of the six villagers for three consecutive moves. The government had to prevent the insurgents winning; and the villagers had simply to survive. It was voted a failure because by concentrating on the food question it failed to introduce the question of terrorism.

The second play was more successful. Considerations of food were eliminated, and attention focused on acts of terrorism, impressment, and military engagement. To provide a more realistic representation of communications, the players were spread out in two rooms and contact made through open doors and by eavesdropping. Uncertainty was added by keeping secret the size of the initial insurgent forces. The criteria for winning were also changed. Thus the insurgents, to win, had to keep the loyalty of 40 percent of the villagers for three consecutive moves and to increase their own starting forces by 20 percent. The government, to win, had to reduce the insurgents by a similar percentage and to keep the loyalty of 80 percent of the villagers. The villagers were divided into three or more villages, and the winning village was that which suffered the smallest population loss while having its loyalty on the right side at the end of the game.

The third play imposed constraints on the belligerents, such as a two-move training delay before impressed villagers could fight for either side. It also introduced the role of a government administrator who provided the government with accurate information about the village. But the administrator could be killed by the insurgents, or by the villagers themselves. Subsequent plays introduced rules for electing a village chief, desertion rates for belligerent forces, and other refinements. By the fifteenth play the game had moved outdoors and messages were delivered by a courier system that was supposed to introduce the kind of delays that might be found in the field. There were also provisions for conflict within villages, military engagements with different degrees of surprise, the calculation of casualties, ambushes, counterambushes, the making of propaganda, and so on. Each game was diligently analyzed to learn more about the interactions of various elements; and switches of loyalty were monitored by means of "villager report forms," filled out after each move and containing questions such as "Who do you want to win?" "Who do you *think* is winning?" and "How do you estimate the loyalties of the rest of your village?"

The manual version of AGILE was later adopted as a counterinsurgency training exercise in Army and Special Forces schools, where it was said to provide "high player involvement" and to teach officers the penalties of neglecting to allow for the political consequences of military actions. But this was a by-product. In the ARPA project it was merely a stage towards developing the computer model.

When the Abt social scientists came to this second part of

their task, they began by converting the manual game into flow charts, suitable for programming. How this was done is illustrated by Figure 5, which is a simplified flow chart based on Abt's original one.[1] This, however, shows only the "gross decision logic" for the simulation. To cover interactions in the game it was necessary to add detailed "routines." For example, the routine for a belligerent planning a game move had to cover the preparation of a list of villages to be visited, the number of men assigned to visit each village, and the purpose of the visit. The elements of this list were determined by what the belligerent perceived to be necessary to his victory—shifts in loyalty, changes in relative force levels, or both. The belligerent then selected actions and villages which tended to satisfy his perceived needs. (In the computer simulation the desirable actions were given numerical "weights" which would induce him—or the computer—to choose the most effective ones.) If the belligerent perceived that he needed a change in force levels to secure victory in a particular village, he had to decide whether to increase his own forces, by recruiting or impressment, or to decrease his opponent's, by ambush or counterambush. If he perceived that he needed a change in the village's loyalty, a routine similar to that in Figure 6 was invoked.

Many other routines were involved in AGILE, as the flow chart indicates. Among them were routines for a village deciding whether to tell a belligerent about an ambush, for deciding whether to resist a belligerent's entry, for determining the "political cohesiveness" of a village, for electing village chiefs, and so on. There was also a "fight routine," which was in some ways the simplest since it resembled the routine in any tactical war game.

However, as we saw with earlier computer games, it was one thing to prepare flow charts and another to translate them into a program. In the case of AGILE one problem was

[1] Abt Associates, Inc., Counter-Insurgency Game Design Feasibility and Evaluation Study, 1965.

AGILE-COIN GROSS DECISION LOGIC

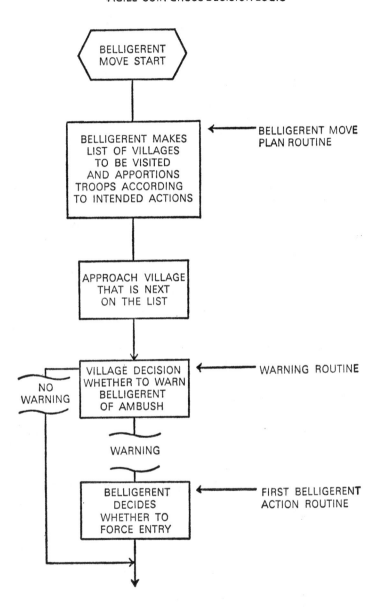

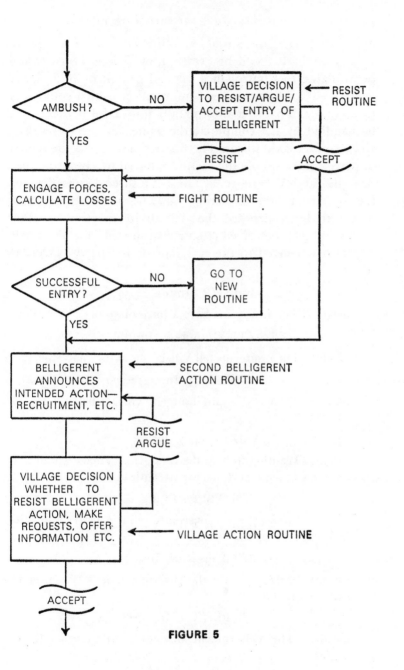

FIGURE 5

how to describe the variables. "Information" could be of several kinds. It could be "real" information (which would be available to Control in a manual game); or it could be "perceived" or "transmitted" information, which could vary in accuracy. To bring information into a form that could be handled by the computer, the game designers used five- and six-letter code words. The first letter denoted the sender or perceiver, or simply the "actor" referred to. (B meant "belligerent" and V "village.") The next three letters denoted the content of the information, e.g., SIZ meant size of forces. The fifth letter denoted the class of information, whether it was real (R), perceived (P), or transmitted (T). The sixth, if present, referred to the recipient or the party perceived. Thus

BSIZR (Insurg) = 50

meant: "The insurgents have a force of 50 men."

BSIZTV (Insurg—3, Insurg) = 70

meant: "The insurgents tell Village 3 that they have 70 men."

VSIZPB (3, Insurg) = 70

meant: "Village 3, a pro-insurgent village, believes the insurgents."

VSIZTV (3, 7, Insurg) = 80

meant: "Wanting to help the insurgents, Village 3 transmits an exaggerated report of their strength to Village 7."

VSIZPB (7, Insurg) = 55

meant: "Village 7, a pro-government village, places little faith in Village 3's report."

VSIZTB (7—Gov, Insurg) = 55

meant: "Village 7 gives the government its estimate of insurgent strength."

BSIZPB (Gov, Insurg) = 52

meant: "The Government discounts Village 7's estimate slightly."

Using this method the computer could handle "information" quite neatly. One of the other two variables, "effective military force," could also be handled quite easily since it was physical and quantifiable. But there was still the last variable —"loyalty." The game designers dealt with this intangible in an ingenious but (inevitably) mechanical way. They defined a village's loyalty as the product of a number of numerically assessed factors: the level of its previous loyalty, its perception of the size of the belligerent forces, its perception of information transmitted by other villages, actions by the belligerents in the village, the application of terror, and so on. All these factors were gathered into an equation which gave a numerical "loyalty rating" for the village, dependent on the values or "weights" assigned to them.

When the game came to be run, the computer performed two tasks. On one hand it played the various actors in the game, exaggerating, understanding, or telling the truth as the logic of the situation demanded. On the other hand, being provided with all the "real information" that in a manual game would be given to Control, it determined, objectively, the outcome of each event, and the result of the game as a whole.

All this may seem very artificial. But the designers of the game, having contrived a program, proceeded to "validate" it in a series of plays in which human actors took part in a Socratic dialogue with the computer, the latter presenting them with specific choices of action. The choices they made corresponded with those which the computer made when acting on its own. In the end the designers decided that the computer was indeed a feasible means of representing the problems of insurgency, because of the speed with which it could assimilate information, and the ease with which one could put in different sets of variables and investigate their effect on the outcome. But they also decided that for both pure and applied research a better method at present was a combination of men and machines, using the Socratic dia-

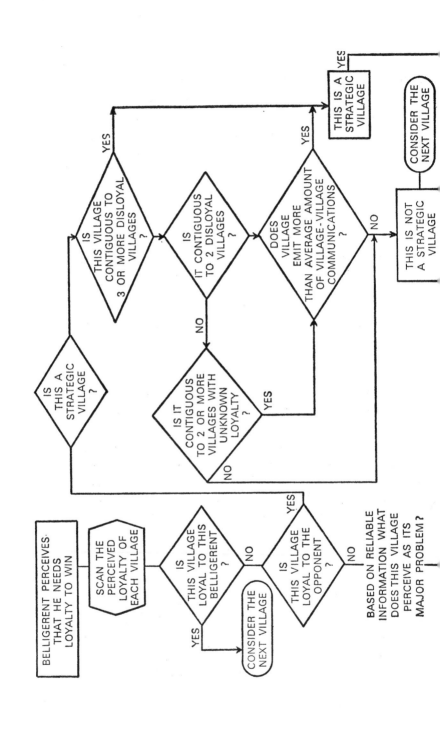

BELLIGERENT PERCEIVES. THAT HE NEEDS LOYALTY TO WIN

SCAN THE PERCEIVED LOYALTY OF EACH VILLAGE

IS THIS VILLAGE LOYAL TO THIS BELLIGERENT ?

CONSIDER THE NEXT VILLAGE

IS THIS VILLAGE LOYAL TO THE OPPONENT ?

BASED ON RELIABLE INFORMATION WHAT DOES THIS VILLAGE PERCEIVE AS ITS MAJOR PROBLEM ?

IS THIS A STRATEGIC VILLAGE ?

IS THIS VILLAGE CONTIGUOUS TO 3 OR MORE DISLOYAL VILLAGES ?

IS IT CONTIGUOUS TO 2 DISLOYAL VILLAGES ?

IS IT CONTIGUOUS TO 2 OR MORE VILLAGES WITH UNKNOWN LOYALTY ?

DOES VILLAGE EMIT MORE THAN AVERAGE AMOUNT OF VILLAGE-VILLAGE COMMUNICATIONS ?

THIS IS A STRATEGIC VILLAGE

CONSIDER THE NEXT VILLAGE

THIS IS NOT A STRATEGIC VILLAGE

YES NO

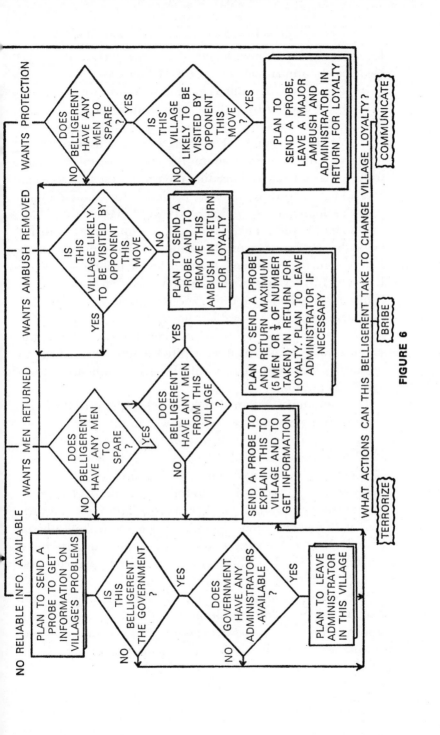

FIGURE 6

WHAT ACTIONS CAN THIS BELLIGERENT TAKE TO CHANGE VILLAGE LOYALTY?

logue method just mentioned, since this preserved a vital element of "human behavioral interaction." [2]

In 1965 a somewhat different kind of Southeast Asian simulation was devised by two scientists of the Douglas Aircraft Corporation, Janice and William Fain, with the title "The 1972 War in Thailand." The scenario was as follows:

In 1972 the Chinese communists, having established control over Cambodia and needing the tin, tungsten, lead, coal, and rubber deposits of the Thai peninsula for Chinese industrial development, assembled a striking force on the Thai–Cambodian border. Their strategy was a four-pronged thrust through the lower central section of Thailand, towards Bangkok in the south and the airfields of Khorat and Koke Kathiem further north. The action was timed to start in February, at which time the dry season would have hardened the inland roads and would last until early May. If the attack could be completed by then, the communists argued, the summer rains would hamper United States–Thai efforts to regain the area, and there would be five months to consolidate their position.

The communists assigned eighty-five battalions to the operation, a strong enough force to overwhelm the Thai defenses if no American forces were involved. Forty-three battalions attacked at the outset and the rest crossed the border during the next twenty-four days. Of the initial attacking force, the larger part struck through the lower region towards Bangkok; the remainder started further north, attacking towards Khorat. Three days later, the units assigned to Koke Kathiem started along the northern route, with the southern force starting after six days. The terrain comprised open country, mountains, forests, swamps, and waterways.

The first units to arrive in the vicinities of Bangkok and Khorat took up holding positions to wait for the rest of their groups before making the final assault. But the units assigned to Koke Kathiem advanced on their objective directly.

[2] *Ibid.*

Of the twenty-two Thai battalions available in the area, ten were assigned to defend Bangkok and the two airfields, and the rest were placed initially along the Cambodian border with planned routes of retreat. The crucial element in the war was the American forces, consisting of three augmented infantry divisions, each of 18,000 men including support troops. The simulation allowed five different timetables for the commitment of the American forces, plus a "basic" situation in which they were not committed at all.

One of the first problems in translating the "war" into a computer simulation was the representation of terrain. This was done by converting features such as forest, swamps, and mountains into one or more rectangular shapes which could be written into a computer program by figures indicating their shape, size, and map coordinates. It was then possible to assign rates of movement of various types of units passing through them. Rivers and canals were represented by crossing points on the planned invasion routes. If a unit had to build a bridge, the program delayed it an hour, or up to twelve hours in the case of resistance.

Units in combat were treated as undergoing a continuous process of attrition whose rate was determined by Lanchester-type equations (see page 46), i.e., they suffered casualties in proportion to the firepower directed against them. The firepower available to each unit was considered to be proportional to its strength, and all available firepower was directed against its various opponents. Attrition rates varied according to both the type of unit and the type of terrain. For example, in open country attacking infantry lost 12 percent of their strength per day of close combat with enemy infantry, and 40 percent per day of bombardment by enemy support artillery. In forests and mountains the rates were diminished because of the effect of concealment.

When the strength of a unit dropped to a certain level, it was assumed to break up and the program eliminated it, at the same time releasing the units it had been fighting and recalculating their movement and attrition rates. When the attrition rate of a defensive unit exceeded a preset figure, a retreat was scheduled. Alternatively a whole group of defensive units could be made to retreat when the offensive force penetrated a certain area.

As a means of monitoring the course of the war, two types of output report were printed. The first, printed at fixed intervals, showed the current strength, movement rate, and attrition rate of each unit; its distance from its objective; and a list of the units with which it was engaged. The second type of report was a record of every event that had occurred. An entire history took about seventy-five output pages.

According to the designers, the game was not intended primarily to study tactics but to determine the effect on the outcome of the "war" of the various timetables for American force commitment. A play of the "basic" situation (in which *no* American forces were committed) resulted in a military disaster for the Thais. The communists moved rapidly on their objectives, reaching all three within twenty-six days. Khorat, the closest, was taken on D plus 12 after a week-long buildup and an attack of only five hours. The attack on Bangkok followed the same general pattern, the city being taken on D plus 26. The Thais were able to offer no really effective resistance, and by the sixteenth day had retreated to their last defense positions in the north. In the case of Koke Kathiem, the communists reached their objective with 94 percent of their original strength. It was thought doubtful whether in this case the war would actually last the forty days covered by the simulation, as the Thais were likely to accept a cease-fire and the setting up of a communist puppet government in Bangkok.

In the second situation (no United States forces committed until D plus 16, then a rapid deployment by D plus 26) the Americans were too late to affect the battle for Khorat but managed to delay the communists' capture of Bangkok by a week. In addition the communists lost twice as many men in the force attacking Bangkok, while the force attacking Koke Kathiem was down, by D plus 40, to a fifth of its starting strength.

In the third situation (United States intervention on D plus 1, but a very slow buildup taking thirty days) the Americans were again unable to save Khorat, but reduced the forces attacking Bangkok to one battalion and wiped out the force attacking Koke Kathiem entirely. The fourth and fifth situations, envisaging only slightly accelerated versions of the American deployment in case 3, produced roughly the same result.

The real payoff, according to the computer results, was in situation number six (the fastest of all American deployments, begun on D plus 1 and completed by D plus 15). Less than 40 percent of the assigned communist force reached Khorat, and no offensive forces reached Bangkok or Koke Kathiem at all. A graph plot of day-to-day computer reports showed that after D plus 20 the communists took exceptionally heavy casualties, and that after D plus 30 the United States–Thai force had a rising superiority of more than 2 to 1. In these circumstances it was thought probable that "the offensive forces would withdraw from Thailand . . . since the few remaining forces could not withstand a United States–Thai counterattack."

Thanks to the voluminous computer output the results of the Thailand War game can be analyzed in considerable detail. Pages of figures show the distance of offensive forces from their objectives, the daily percentage of combat losses, the ratio of forces committed, and variations of the force ratio with time. (For good measure the final report includes the complete game history of a Chinese infantry battalion.) But to what do all these figures refer?—Six variations of a synthetic war fought on gross assumptions and in highly contrived conditions. In every engagement the deciding factor is the crude one of firepower. Intangibles are omitted. The performance of fighting units is held constant. There is no

role for surprise, because the computer "knows everything."
The greatest artificiality of all is that there is no dynamic
mechanism whereby one side may freely react, by changes of
plan, to the actions of the other.

The most interesting question the Thailand War game
raises is the deductions which might be drawn from its
results. These point to one thing: the importance of an adequate airlift capability for the American forces, because airlift
would be virtually the only means of increasing the speed
of an American deployment in the theater under consideration. Of course the advantages of a good airlift capability
in a situation such as this are almost too obvious to need
mention. But what the simulation does *not* prove is the
further conclusion that the unwary might draw from it—
that by an increased investment in the products of the aerospace industry the United States could ensure the security
of Thailand and avoid another Vietnam.

More ambitious than AGILE or the Thailand War game
is a computer model called TEMPER (Technological, Economic, Military, Political Evaluation Routine). Starting in
1962 from what was modestly described as an attempt to
demonstrate a theory of international relations, TEMPER
grew up into a model that now professes to simulate just
about everything from the interactions of thirty-nine states
in the Cold War to a nuclear exchange between two blocs
in a "hot" one. It was designed by the Raytheon company,
which is a major contractor in the military electronics business. The leading designer was Clark Abt, later the founder
of Abt Associates, which may explain some similarities with
AGILE. Though critically regarded by a majority of military
war gamers, TEMPER represents an ideal goal for some
Pentagon computer enthusiasts who believe that, with time,
all military problems will be open to analysis.

The world of TEMPER consists of some twenty "conflict
regions," each with assumed political alignments, economic

resources and military capabilities. The model is said to be able to sense discrepancies between the "real world" and the ideal world which the leaders of each region would like to see. It then makes the most cost-effective choice of action, carries out the operation (an investment in a weapons system, or an attack on an opponent), and adjusts the world accordingly.

In each cycle, the model must "trade off" competing demands on the resources of each country or region. For example, in the trade-off of domestic and military needs, the military budget competes with foreign aid, foreign trade, and domestic investment needs. Depending on the threat perceived, military spending goes up or down. Military actions are determined by enemy actions and the posture of the model. There is also an alliance routine, in which an ally can call for help. Whether he is helped depends on his past performance as an ally, his value as an ally, and whether he and the country appealed to share common objectives. There is also a trade-off between research-and-development and production budgets, and between military quality and quantity.

Using a mixture of manual and machine play, early runs of TEMPER took thirty–forty minutes to simulate about ten years of world operations. Later this was improved. But it was still felt that it took too long to train people to use the model. The goal was to have a cathode-ray or similar display system which would make it possible for a novice to learn to play in five or ten minutes. "What we would like some day," Abt once told an Inter-Agency group on strategic studies, "is a system with fifteen buttons, five for each of the military political functions. One button might control the variable the user wanted to operate on, another might control the geographic regions, and so on. With a few dials and a map display it might then be possible to represent most of the complexities of the model."

When last heard of, the designers of TEMPER were working on a "technical force requirements model" to remedy inadequacies at the general war end of its range of capability. The improved model was intended to endow it with the ability to choose the best "mix" of strategic and tactical forces, missiles and bombers, carriers and submarines, etc. At the finest level of resolution it was expected to be possible to break down the intercontinental missile force into four dominant characteristics—survivability, kill potential, damage-limiting capability (i.e., ability to destroy enemy missile sites), and targeting flexibility. Each of these would then be broken down again into its component elements; for example, kill potential would be broken down into the best mix of range, accuracy, payload, etc. Costs and marginal utilities would then be used to determine the optimum choice of weapon. The designers hoped it would thus be possible to fight a general war "not through just one cycle of attack and retaliation, but through as many cycles as are needed to reach some termination criterion."

The purpose of all these games is pure or applied research. Pure research is generally defined, in the military sphere, as an attempt to gain a fuller understanding of political or military interactions; applied research ranges from "data collection" to the assessment of alternative strategies and the identification of "indicators" by which to judge the probable results of current operations. But there is another type of game, both manual and mechanized, which aspires to a headier kind of research—the generation of "possible futures." If one asks why war games are necessary for this purpose, which in its time has been ably accomplished without them by Jules Verne, H. G. Wells, and other science-fiction writers, the professional answer is that although plausible scenarios can be produced by a fertile imagination, "method" is necessary to produce scenarios whose development from the present can be traced in scientific detail.

The pioneer of scenario generation was Herman Kahn, and the work he did in the 1950s is reflected in Chapter 10 of *On Thermonuclear War*. Kahn, however, used seminar gaming methods. The computer method was only developed ten years later when the U.S. Air Force Systems Command decided that the generation of a wide range of possible scenarios was necessary for space operations study. This was because of the long time required to plan space systems (fifteen to twenty years) compared with other advanced systems. The Air Force adopted computer games in the belief the computer was free from the inhibitions and prejudices inseparable from human thinking.

The first step in preparing the ground for a computer game was to draw up a list of all the nations which might be capable of developing space capabilities by 1985. On the basis of predicted increases of gross national product and liability to strategic involvement in global politics, the list prepared by the Air Force consultant [3] came to forty-two countries, headed by the United States and completed by the Congo. Current relations between these countries were then projected into the future using the criterion of geopolitical distance—that is to say, geopolitically close countries such as the U.S. and Britain, or Germany and France, were deemed likely to undergo more dramatic changes in their current relationship than countries like Australia and Mexico. A six-point scale was then constructed to represent the hierarchy of relations between nation-pairs, ranging from one point for political-military alliance to six points for maximum hostility. Since each nation was considered capable of sliding the full length of five units during the twenty-year period considered, there were theoretically five [4] future alliance patterns that could be derived from current values. However, since it was assumed that the present four principal "space actors" (America, Rus-

[3] S. A. Bornstein, "A Scenario Generation Methodology," prepared for SPAD Management Office DCS/Plans, HQ, Air Force Systems Cmd., Washington, D.C. (mimeo), Abt Associates, Inc., Cambridge, Mass., 1966.
[4] M. Fuchida and M. Okumiya, *Midway, the Battle that Doomed Japan* (London: Hutchinson, 1957).

sia, China, and Western Europe) would continue to dominate the space scene during the period, it was found possible to group future worlds into four types and fifteen subtypes defined by the alliance structures of these four space leaders.

Combining the four blocs into their possible alliance arrangements yielded fifteen possibilities, of which two (Europe versus an alliance of America, Russia, and China, and Russia and America independently opposing a European-Chinese alliance) were eliminated as politically improbable. To allow for the possibility of an entirely new set of power blocs coming into being before 1985 a "wild card" world type was added to the list, which is given in Figure 7.

When it came to devising the scenario-generating computer model, a number of manually derived scenarios were examined to discover the variables most sensitive to a crisis. These were found to be international relations, trade relations, arms postures, national policies, and levels of conflict. ("National policies" were compounded from two separate variables: the values set by a state on national survival and the fulfillment of national aspirations respectively.) Each variable was given a scale index. In the case of bilateral variables—international relations, trade relations, and arms postures—the scale was based on "degree of competitiveness." Thus in international relations, as we have seen, a political-military alliance with another country rated 1 on the scale; a political alliance 2; neutrality 3; policy conflicts 4; strong hostility 5; and total enmity 6. Trade relations followed a similar index. The arms posture index went from 1 (receiving arms support) to 9 (engaged in an arms race with the other country). The foreign policy scale of values, representing national aspirations, went from 1 to 6 through "isolation," "peaceful coexistence," "containment," "peaceful expansion," "*forceful* expansion," and "alien reduction" (the defeat of other countries). Additional devices were provided for representing the outcomes of wars in terms of casualties and "the dollar value of daily damage."

Once again the preliminary step towards constructing a computer game model was the playing of a manual game, in this case called SPARC (Space Planning Against Ranged Contingencies). The players consisted of a control team and a number of "national" teams responsible for designing space systems that were technologically and financially feasible and within their countries' interests. Play began with a distribution of "space arsenals," budgets, projected capability ranges, etc. After this the nation teams convened one-hour planning sessions, representing three to four years of real time, to develop space systems that met their military objectives. At the

---

World Type I: "One World"
            1985—U.S./U.S.S.R./Europe/China

World Type II: "Three and One"
            1977—IIA: U.S.—U.S.S.R./Europe/China
            1981—IIB: U.S.S.R.—U.S./Europe/China
              —   IIC: Europe—U.S./U.S.S.R./China (eliminated)
            1976—IID: China—U.S./U.S.S.R./Europe

World Type III: "Two and Two"
            1978—IIIA: U.S./U.S.S.R.—Europe/China
            1973—IIIB: U.S./Europe—U.S.S.R./China
            1980—IIIC: U.S./China—U.S.S.R./Europe

World Type IV: "Two and One and One"
            1979—IVA: U.S./U.S.S.R.—Europe—China
            1974—IVB: U.S./Europe—U.S.S.R.—China
            1972—IVC: U.S./China—U.S.S.R.—Europe
            1982—IVD: U.S.S.R./Europe—U.S.—China
            1983—IVE: U.S.S.R./China—U.S.—Europe
              —   IVF: Europe/China—U.S.—U.S.S.R. (eliminated)

World Type V: "Multipolarity"
            1975—U.S.—U.S.S.R.—Europe—China

World Type VI: "Wild Card"
            1984—Examples:
                        Rich—Poor
                        White—Colored
                        Wars of Religion

───────── FIGURE 7 ─────────

end of the first session, the nation teams submitted their completed systems to Control. After checking the systems for feasibility, and making any necessary modifications, Control gave out a "decision-critical" situation that would necessitate changes in national space missions. Then there would be another one-hour planning session; and so on. Cost guidelines gave a tariff for basic hardware items, ranging from $2 million for a simple Atlas intercontinental rocket without warhead to $30 million for putting an H-bomb into high orbit.

In the computer game the variables were given ranges and units of measurement for mechanical classification. To avoid human bias in the assignment of exact values to the variables, the program was designed to select such values at random within the given ranges. The detailed situations were then given a first computer run; and if the outcome seemed unfeasible, the reason was checked and the program modified. The whole thing was then given a second run, modified again if necessary, and given a series of runs. The same "iteration" procedure was then carried through for other scenarios, until the resulting computer program was considered effective.

What may strike the layman as more interesting than the mechanics of the game are some of the "worlds" generated during its development. For example a world of Type Two (three power blocs against one) about 1977 contained an increasingly isolationist and militant America confronted by an alliance of the other major powers, Russia, Europe and China. Britain, however, had sided with the United States, as had Canada. America had three armed space stations, and an unarmed base on the moon. Russia and a reunified Germany had jointly developed similar capabilities. France, opposed to both America and the Russian-German alliance, had reconnaissance satellites and long-range nuclear rockets; but being more hostile to America than to Russia and Germany, supported Russia and Germany diplomatically as a result of the 1974 Alliance of Cannes. The northern European nations, except the "neutral" Scandinavians and Switzerland, were allied with Russia and Germany, and the southern European nations with France. China, with fairly advanced space capabilities, was master of Asia. In Latin America, the Organization of American States had collapsed; Guatemala had become openly pro-communist and Mexico was flirting with the European-Soviet bloc. Most Latin-American countries, except Brazil, were neutral or hostile to the United States. Elsewhere America's only strong allies were Australia and Japan, in both of which countries the United States had missile sites. South Africa, the only pro-American country in Africa, fell to "native insurgents" in 1972. "Decision-critical" events given out by Control included a Russian-German start on building missile bases in Mexico, an Anglo-German shooting match over North Sea oil rigs, and the fall of the Brazilian government to communist revolutionaries.

Another Type Two world, about 1981, saw Russia ranged against America, Europe, and China, after America, about 1969, had "surgically removed" Chinese nuclear capacity and set up a pro-American government in Peking.

A world of Type Three (described as a "two and two" world) about 1978 foresaw the disintegration of NATO in 1969 followed by an American–Soviet nonaggression pact "over the heads" of the European countries. In the early 1970s a French-led Europe, including Britain and a nuclear reunified Germany, moved towards an alliance with Peking as a means of escaping encirclement by the Washington–Moscow bloc. The alliance was finally concluded, leaving the world divided between the Washington–Moscow and Paris–Peking blocs. Japan, playing both ends against the middle, was allied with both Russia and China, while India was courting both but allied to neither. Latin America had formed a regional defense pact excluding the United States and, led by Brazil, had become an independent force in world politics. The Middle Eastern countries favored the Paris–

Peking axis, except Israel, which was allied with the Washington–Moscow axis. Black governments had controlled all Africa south of the Sahara since 1974.

Among sample decision-critical situations were a West German–Chinese attack on the Soviet Union, and an offer by the Congo to accept an American–Russian missile base on its territory.

There was also a Type Four world ("two and one and one") in which a softening of Chinese ideology, combined with a purge of "Kosyginite deviationists" in Moscow, had led to a Chinese–Russian rapproachement, while America and Europe had drifted apart as a result of the European Common Market and Europe's resurgence as a world power. Another "two and one and one" world envisaged a Russian–European alliance, following "liberalization" in Russia and, in 1978, a Russo–European nonaggression pact. In this world there was an isolationist America and expansionist China. Mexico and Canada were cooperating with the United States in developing a manned base on the moon, and the Russian–European bloc was not far behind. The Russian–European block was competing with China in Africa, while America was preoccupied with a disorganized, nuclear, and largely hostile Latin America.

Among the critical situations derived from this scenario was one in which China inspired a bombing attack on South Africa from the Congo and threatened nuclear retaliation against anyone who intervened. Subsequently a Russian-inspired counterrevolution brought Chinese troops to the Congo, with the result that neighboring countries, under Russian–European influence, threatened military action if the Chinese did not leave.

A Type Five ("multipolar") world, about 1975, saw all four power groups in some form of competition, with a tense situation in Europe as a result of the buildup of a Franco–German axis "known popularly in Germany as the 'Fourth Reich.'" Britain, allied with the Netherlands, Sweden, Finland, Norway, and Denmark, and sharing her fairly advanced space capabilities with this "Outer Europe," was trying to improve Soviet–American relations and get the United States and Russia to clamp down on the "Fourth Reich." Critical situations envisaged by the scenario included marches by the Fourth Reich into East Germany and the Netherlands.

The antithesis of Type Five was the Type One world, in which, about 1985, there was world government with its own armed forces and a stockpile of 100 intercontinental missiles. It had two armed space stations, an unarmed scientific base on the moon, and was in process of establishing a similar base on Mars.

But the raciest example, as might be expected, was a Type Six ("wild card") world, envisaged about 1984. In this, India, Africa, and China had been caught up since 1975 by a new religion called Muluism, whose basic tenet was the evil of the white man. South Africa had been clear of whites since a bloody war in 1978 costing millions of lives. South of the Sahara a "black African Federation" possessed several dozen nuclear-armed intermediate range missiles left over from prewar days, and a huge ten-million-strong army equipped with little more than spears. In Asia the Muluist Coalition had demanded the departure of all whites by 1984, and appeared ready to kill all who did not comply. Japan, only partly under the influence of Muluism, was torn internally and expected to have a Muluist majority within a few years. America, Russia, and Europe were united in a loose economic federation, with varying political relationships among them. Australia and Canada were allied with the developed countries, as was also South America, though the latter had scattered Muluist pockets. In the United States about four million out of thirty million Negroes had espoused Muluism, and there had been riots in the South and in northern city ghettos. Washington, with an 83-percent colored population, had been under martial law for a year. The Republican party, long out of office, was demanding a "get tough quick" policy against the "Mulu menace," and was expected to win the coming elections by a landslide.

Crisis situations arising from the scenario envisaged an Indian fanatic firing a nuclear missile at Leningrad after Russian "provocation" against Muluist Afghanistan, a march by Muluist armies to take over the remainder of Africa, a call for American and Soviet help to put down a Muluist revolution in Japan, and the outbreak of widespread rioting in the southern United States.

Enough things have happened since 1966, when the above scenarios were "generated," to discourage the observation that any of them are necessarily implausible—the sacking of American cities by Negro rioters, a left-wing student revolt in Europe, the deployment of American defenses against Chinese rockets, to name just a few. But although futuristic war games may serve to remind us that the world is not fixed in its present shape forever, they remain, for all their "method," no more than leaps in the dark. Because of the variety of the futures they demonstrate, they can give little help in planning the future—and could well saddle us with neuroses more dangerous than the threats they appear to expose. Above all, if taken seriously, they could lead us to even heavier investment than at present in deterrent systems, at the cost of human needs less easily dramatized.

A quite different approach to the problem of the unknown, since it deals entirely in the abstract, is that of "game theory," which we shall now examine. The American use of it for the practical analysis of operational problems has caused great misgivings among European scientists such as Blackett and Zuckerman. But, as we shall see, game theory can also illuminate the predicament into which other types of analysis have led us.

10

GAME THEORY[1]

THE "THEORY OF GAMES," or game theory, has nothing to do
with war games as we have described them so far. The games
to which it refers are theoretical models derived from games
of chance. In these, as in bridge or poker, each player has
some control over the outcome of the game; but not full
control, because the other players, and chance, will also influence events. However, it will readily be seen that this description fits numerous military situations also; and many
people believe that game theory is relevant to the study (or
even the practice) of politico-military strategy.

About 300 years ago the mathematical study of games of
chance led to the theory of probability. But it was not until
1928 that an American mathematician, John von Neumann,
succeeded in constructing a theory based on their strategic

[1] The attempt in this chapter to explain the rudiments of game theory is
largely based on Professor Anatol Rapoport's *Strategy and Conscience*, published by Harper & Row, 1964.

element. Neumann went on to develop this theory with a Princeton colleague, Oskar Morgenstern, and in 1944 they published a joint work [2] which identified factors common to both games and economics. Subsequently both became involved with the development of weapons in the United States, Neumann becoming chairman of the committee which specified the design of the first American intercontinental ballistic missile.

The key to Neumann's theory was his concept of strategy. By this he meant a player's method of playing a game from start to finish. The combination of each player's strategy determined the outcome of the game, which Neumann measured in terms of a "payoff" to each player. The object of the theory was to show what would be the optimal strategy for each player.

In its simplest form, game theory can be applied to a situation of pure competition involving only two players. In it, each of the players, A and B, chooses a strategy from a limited number of possibilities without knowing the strategy the other is choosing. The payoff he receives can be positive, negative, or zero, according to whether he wins, loses, or draws. In this way the game can be represented by a rectangular array of numbers called a payoff matrix (see Figure 8) in which each horizontal row corresponds to a strategy for A, and each vertical column to a strategy for B. The numbers in each square show the payoff from A to B and from B to A that a combination of the strategies "intersecting" in that square would produce. (Since A's gain is B's loss and vice versa it is not really necessary to show the payoff B receives; but when this is done, B's payoff is generally shown in the top right-hand corner of the square, and A's in the opposite corner.)

In games of pure competition or conflict, game theory teaches that A, to ensure the best results for himself, must

[2] John von Neumann and Oskar Morgenstern, *Theory of Games and Economic Behavior*, 2nd edition (Princeton, N.J.: Princeton University Press, 1947).

assess each strategy by the gain it will give him *regardless of what B may do.* In other words, he must pessimistically assume that B knows his plan and will counter it so as to limit his gain to a minimum. Another way of expressing this is to say that A must maximize his *assured* gain; or, again, that he must make as great as possible the least gain to which B can limit him. This maximization of the minimum is sometimes called the max-min. In terms of the payoff matrix it is achieved by choosing the row in which the least entry is greatest. B, on the other hand, must choose the strategy which minimizes the greatest loss that A can inflict. This is known as the min-max and is achieved by choosing the column in which the greatest entry is least. Clearly A's max-min payoff cannot be greater than B's min-max payoff; but the two can be equal—and when this happens there is an entry in the matrix which is both least in its row and the greatest in its column. Such an entry is called the *minimax* or "saddleback."

Now, it has been pointed out [3] that games of pure competition or conflict (generally called *zero-sum* games, because the sum of one side's gain and the other's loss will always be 0) can be divided into those which have a minimax and those which do not. Those with a minimax are less complex and can be divided into three groups:

(1) games in which both players have what is called a "dominating strategy"
(2) games in which only one player has a dominating strategy
(3) games in which neither player has a dominating strategy.

A dominating strategy is one whose outcomes are better than, or at least as good as, the corresponding outcomes of any other possible strategy.

An example of a game in which both sides have a dominating strategy is represented by the matrix in Figure 8, in

[3] Rapoport, *op. cit.*

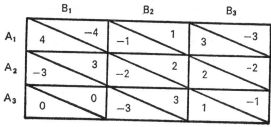

	B_1	B_2	B_3
A_1	4 / −4	−1 / 1	3 / −3
A_2	0 / 0	−2 / 2	2 / −2
A_3	0 / 0	−3 / 3	1 / −1

FIGURE 8

which rows A_1, A_2, and A_3 are the strategies available to A, and the columns B_1, B_2, and B_3 are the strategies open to B. (To make the diagram explicit, the payoffs to both players are given.) In this game, strategy A_1 dominates strategies A_2 and A_3 because whatever strategy B chooses, A is at least as well off, and sometimes better off, with A_1 than with either of the others. B is in a similar position with *his* dominating strategy, B_2.

Now, if the position is slightly altered as in Figure 9, only A has a dominating strategy, because B has to take account of what A may do before knowing whether B_2 is best. For example, if A were to choose A_2, B would be worse off with B_2 than with B_1. However, by looking at the matrix B can know that A, as a rational being, will still choose A_1, since his advantage in doing so is unchanged.

Figure 10 illustrates the third type of possibility in a two-player zero-sum game, namely that in which neither side has a dominating strategy. For, as the reader will see, a row giving good results in conjunction with one column, will produce

	B_1	B_2	B_3
A_1	4 / −4	−1 / 1	3 / −3
A_2	−3 / 3	−2 / 2	2 / −2
A_3	0 / 0	−3 / 3	1 / −1

FIGURE 9

poor results in conjunction with another, and the same will happen with columns in regard to rows. In a game of this type it is not possible for either player to arrive at a rational choice of strategy without taking account of the other's decision process. And this means not merely taking account of the other's choice preferences (as happened with B in our previous example) but also taking account of the other's taking account of one's own choice preferences, as well as one's taking account of the other's taking account, etc., ad infinitum.

This is where the importance of the minimax comes in. For if the game has a minimax position, it is to this combination of strategies that the reasoning of both sides must eventually lead. In Figure 10 the minimax is yielded by a combination of A_1 and B_2—a payoff to A of −1 and to B of 1. Admittedly this is the worst payoff to A in that row, but it is better than the worst payoffs in the other two rows. Similarly, B's payoff is the poorest in that column, but it is better than the two other worst payoffs.

If a game has no minimax, it becomes impossible for either player to know what the other will do. In this case—or rather in the case of a series of such games—game theory prescribes the use of "randomized" or "mixed" strategies, that is to say, the use now of one strategy, now of another. The strategy is selected in a random manner from among the available "pure" strategies in accordance with chosen weights. This avoids a uniform pattern, for example a change of strategy

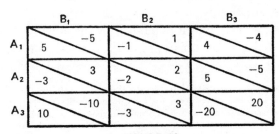

FIGURE 10

every other move, from which an opponent might benefit in the long run. An optimal randomization of strategy could be used in poker, if somebody had the time to work it out, and would mean that in the long run each player would end up with zero winnings and zero losses. Mixed strategies can also be applied, theoretically, to some military choices when these fall within a zero-sum context.

An example is the problem of a commander having to choose between two targets: one of great value but likely to be well defended, the other less important but more open to successful attack. The enemy commander also has a problem: which target to defend more strongly. It might first strike the enemy commander that the more critical target should be more strongly defended. But on second thoughts he must realize that this is what the attacker expects. On this basis he might decide to do the opposite of what the attacker expects, and put his main defenses around the less important target. But then he might reason: Is not the enemy liable to follow my thoughts and direct his attack at the first target? The fact is that both commanders could be going through the same process of reasoning, which could continue indefinitely.

What game theory counsels is that the attacking commander should calculate the optimum long-term distribution of his choices between target A and target B, on the hypothesis that the choice would arise repeatedly. He should then resort to a random number device and act according to the number turned up.[4] The defender, of course, is counseled to do likewise. Naturally, the combination of numbers may lead either side into disaster; the attacker, choosing the minor target, may find it defended; or the defender, uncovering the major target, may present the attacker with a walkover. But at least (says game theory) it will be a *logical*

[4] This method is mechanically similar to the use of random numbers to determine the outcome of an event within the probability percentages specified by rules in tactical war games. A method of calculating the optimal randomization mixtures in games for two players, each with a choice of two strategies, is given in J. D. Williams' *The Compleat Strategyst*.

disaster, and both sides will have acted as intelligently as could be expected of them.

Now, all this may seem bizarre, though in "real life" commanders often do "randomize" their strategy, intuitively, by sometimes resorting to bluff and sometimes to double-bluff. However, for our game-theoretical example to work in the way intended, three conditions are necessary, which, in practice, seldom exist. First, there must be complete secrecy about each side's preparations for the battle. Secondly, each side must be certain that the other is using a random strategy. Thirdly, there must be numerous repetitions of the same basic situation to ensure good results.

These demanding conditions have not deterred some theorists from advocating the use of a randomized strategy, or rather a randomized threat, as a means of nuclear deterrence. For example, it has been suggested that to meet situations where the threat of *automatic* nuclear retaliation lacks credibility a retaliatory mechanism with a built-in fractional chance of actuation could provide greater credibility. Again, though this is bizarre, it has an informal parallel in the American deterrent threat vis-à-vis a Soviet attack on Western Europe. For this, if it serves as a deterrent at all, can no longer be regarded as an *automatic* threat, any more than the threat of British and French nuclear retaliation to Soviet attack could be regarded as 100 percent certain.

But when we come to the study of nuclear strategy and international relations, zero-sum games cease to be a valid model; for, as a moment's reflection will show, the problems here are not problems of pure conflict but problems involving a mixture of conflict and cooperation (to avoid mutual annihilation). The nature of this truth is most ably demonstrated by another game-theoretical model called Prisoner's Dilemma.

In the game's original scenario, two prisoners charged with the same crime are held incommunicado. If both confess, both can be convicted. If neither confesses, neither can be convicted. But if one confesses while the other stays silent, the first not only goes free but gets a reward as well; and the second gets a harsher punishment than he would have got if both had confessed. Should a rational prisoner confess or hold out in these circumstances?

Applied to international relations, Prisoner's Dilemma becomes an attempt to represent the essential features of a deadlock in which two nations are unable to cooperate with each other for want of mutual trust.

Suppose that Red and Blue are aware that each presents a military threat to each other but have a common interest in avoiding war. Each realizes that from the standpoint of its economy it is spending too much on defense and that if each could be secure from attack, its defense budget could be reduced to mutual benefit. In other words, both could be secure regardless of the absolute level of armaments, provided these levels were approximately equal. It follows that in these circumstances it is in the interest of both countries to reduce the arms level or disarm altogether, though both countries recognize that if one disarmed unilaterally it would be at a severe disadvantage. Such a situation is represented by the matrix in Figure 11, in which the advantage of being disarmed is assigned a value of 5, the cost of being armed a value of —5, the strategic advantage of being the only armed state a value of 10, and the strategic disadvantage of being the only disarmed state a value of —10.

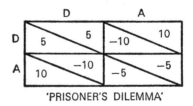

'PRISONER'S DILEMMA'

FIGURE 11

From this matrix it will be seen that strategy A (for "arm") dominates strategy D (for "disarm") for both players. This is because Blue, obeying the game theory, must assume the worst, i.e., that Red chooses A, in which case his own choice of A limits his maximum possible loss to —5, compared with a possible loss of —10 if he were to choose D; and Red must assume the same about Blue. But the matrix also shows that by choosing the dominating strategy (to arm) both do worse than if they had chosen the alternative. This, of course, is a replica of a real world situation which most people will recognize.

One way out of the situation would be for both sides to get together and agree to disarm. But games schematized in matrix form do not allow for such "moves," only for "strategies." Moreover, the prisoners in the original game were incommunicado. Suppose, however, that we discard these formal limitations and consider a real world situation in which communication is possible. There is still the difficulty that neither side can be sure that the other will keep any agreement, and the choice of trusting the other side or not can in fact be represented as a further game of Prisoner's Dilemma.

Prisoner's Dilemma is by no means the only non-zero-sum game. It has achieved a kind of celebrity because it so neatly sums up a situation in which there are two opposed but apparently "rational" choices. Another "2 × 2" game (for two players, each with a choice of two strategies) in the same class is "Chicken." This is classically used to illustrate the principles of nuclear deterrence, and in its physical form, once popular among American teen-agers, consists of two youths driving cars at each other at high speed along a straight line. The loser is the one whose nerve breaks soonest and swerves to avoid a collision. What distinguishes Chicken from Prisoner's Dilemma is the payoffs in the matrix, as Figure 12 shows.

In Chicken the penalty suffered by the two noncooperators (—100 in our example) is greater than that suffered by the solitary cooperator, whereas in Prisoner's Dilemma it is less. What this means in real-life Chicken, whether between teen-agers or between governments which have got themselves into a nuclear confrontation, is that if Blue can convince Red of his resolve *not* to cooperate, Red's only rational choice is to cooperate, i.e., to "swerve," to avoid the —100 penalty. In the language of game theory, the outcomes DA and AD are both "equilibrium" outcomes; neither player can alone move away from either outcome without worsening his payoff. In Prisoner's Dilemma, by contrast, there is only one equilibrium outcome, AA. Thus in Chicken the "rational" incentive to choose a noncooperative strategy is even stronger from one point of view; though, as in Prisoner's Dilemma, it is totally irrational from the overall standpoint.

Although there are no less than seventy-two "2 × 2" games (and tens of thousands of "2 × 3" ones) we need go no further than this to know the background to a bitter debate which has arisen over game theory and its application to foreign policy problems in recent years. In its purely theoretical manifestation the argument concerns an escape from the rational contradictions of the non-zero-sum games mentioned above. The first of the two suggested solutions is that advanced by Thomas Schelling, whom we met in Chapter 4.

In his book *The Strategy of Conflict,* published in 1963, Schelling suggested that provided the two sides in a non-zero-sum situation perceived the long-term advantages of "coordinating their expectations," the problem of communication was not as great as it seemed. This was due to the existence in many situations of what he called a "prominent" solution, which both sides could easily recognize.

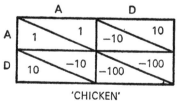

'CHICKEN'

FIGURE 12

"A" means "cooperate"; "D" means "defect."

To illustrate the point Schelling presented the reader with the following problems:

1. Name "heads" or "tails." If you and your partner name the same, you win a prize.
2. You are to meet someone in New York City, but neither you nor the other person are told where. Choose a place which is most likely to coincide with his guess.
3. You are told the date but not the hour of the above meeting. At what time will you appear at the meeting place elected?

It was scarcely necessary for Schelling to try out those problems on a number of people in order to show that "prominent" solutions existed. ("Heads"; "the information booth at Grand Central Station"; "twelve noon.") From this he went on to develop a theory of coordination and tacit bargaining between governments, in peace and in limited war, which has been one of his major contributions to American strategic thinking.

But Schelling's coordination theory was still only a psychological addition to game theory. In real life it showed a means of alleviating international dilemmas if governments were willing. It did not remove the formal contradiction between the two "most reasonable" solutions for either side in any non-zero-sum game.

What promised to be a much bolder solution was that advanced by Anatol Rapoport, a senior research mathematician at the University of Michigan. In his book *Strategy and Conscience,* published a year after Schelling's, Rapoport, who was already a recognized innovator of game theory, suggested that the only way to resolve the rational dichotomy in non-zero-sum games was to elevate "conscience" in such a way as to eliminate the narrower type of "rational solution." By "conscience" Rapoport meant obedience to Kant's categorical imperative—"Act in such a way that the principle of your action could become a universal law"—though the moral authority to whom he appealed was not Kant but Tolstoy.

"The player who chooses [the strategy of cooperation in a Prisoner's Dilemma game]," wrote Rapoport, "does so because he feels it is the proper thing to do. He feels that he ought to behave as he would like the other to behave. He knows that if both behave as he expects, both will benefit. I submit that there are pretty compelling reasons. . . ."

However, as a game theoretician, he was bound to point out that they were not *strategic* reasons. Indeed they contradicted the "rational" strategic principle, which dictated a policy of noncooperation unconditionally.

He then went on to examine the apparent exception to this principle which occurred when Prisoner's Dilemma was played twice, the two plays being "collapsed" into a single supergame in which each player had the choice of not two, but many, strategies. One of these strategies was to say "I shall play cooperatively on the first move; on the second move I shall play as the other has played on the first." Against this strategy of a "just man with an initial reservoir of good will," as Rapoport put it, the other player would do better to cooperate (at least on the first move). But the trouble was that to be safe in playing this strategy, the second player would need to be assured that the first would indeed play the strategy in question, rather than a noncooperative one. "To be sure," said Rapoport, "it is to A's advantage to play the cooperative strategy (against which B would play a cooperative strategy if he was rational), but this would happen only if B *knew* that A had chosen the cooperative strategy."

So the question of communication arose. But unlike Schelling, Rapoport did not see a means of communication as a way out of the dilemma—unless there was a means of enforcing any agreement reached. If a *non*enforceable agreement were made by the players of a single game of Prisoner's Dilemma, he pointed out, the question "Should I keep the pact?" induced another game exactly like Prisoner's Dilemma, and in this game, of the two available strategies, namely to keep the pact or to break it, the strategy of breaking the pact was dominant.

In the end Rapoport concluded that no definition of rationality could be given which would remain intuitively satisfactory for non-zero-sum games in all contexts. Therefore nobody could say how one ought to make decisions in such games without invoking considerations outside game theory, and these considerations frequently belonged to the realm of ethics.

If this were all, *Strategy and Conscience* would merely have been an innovating game theory textbook, unusual for raising ethical questions in what was generally considered a field of purely "scientific" study. But it was not all. Rapoport, who already had strong "peace group" affinities, embarked on his book in white-hot indignation after sitting through a potted version of Herman Kahn's three-day lecture which formed the basis of *On Thermonuclear War*. At the end of the lecture, after hearing Kahn discuss options between counterforce and counter-city targets, he had asked him whether he would agree to a definition of "genocide" as a deliberate slaughter of helpless populations for political ends, and if so how he would defend himself if at some future time he were a co-respondent at a genocide trial. The question, as he himself later admitted, was considered to be in "bad academic form."

The book was an attack, not merely on some aspects of game theory application, but on the whole community of American "strategists": men like Kahn, Henry Kissinger, Klaus Knorr, Albert Wohlstetter, and Schelling, who have undoubtedly had an influence on official policy making. (The inclusion of Schelling in the list was poignant, because in *The Strategy of Conflict* he had gone out of his way to praise an earlier book of Rapoport's, *Fights, Games and Debates*.

He had also been ahead of Rapoport in drawing attention to the non-zero-sum nature of relations between rival power blocs.)

"My critique," wrote Rapoport, "is intended to be more than a critique of a particular policy or strategy. It is directed rather at strategic thinking itself. For although the strategists repeat often and with great emphasis that a nuclear war could spell a loss for both, they nevertheless fall into a conceptual trap of their own making. Recall that although Prisoner's Dilemma is a non-zero-sum game and is readily perceived as such, it is *strategically* indistinguishable from a zero-sum game in which both players have a dominating strategy. This is the zero-sum trap, because it seeks one strategic 'solution,' but there is no strategic escape from the trap." [5]

Rapoport was careful to say that in choosing alternative day-to-day actions in the Cold War, the strategist did not uniformly advocate courses calculated simply to hurt the opponent *in the short run*. That would have clashed too sharply with "current sensibilities." But the zero-sum-game assumption was pronounced in the fact that "we attribute to the *other* preference for those courses of action which are most devastating to ourselves. The fact that the other does not as a rule carry out those actions is attributed almost exclusively to the effectiveness of deterrence." Of course, said Rapoport, the most important of the enemy's potential choices was the nuclear surprise attack (the bogey of which had been resurrected by Herman Kahn); and in the writings of the strategists the "successful" nuclear surprise attack was represented as a winning move of the game. The analogy was obvious. The winning of the game was the ultimate objective, and all other considerations were related to it.

Strategy and Conscience provoked a large number of

[5] *Op. cit.*, page 107.

critical reviews, of which the best, together with Rapoport's published reply to the critics, are almost as interesting as the book itself.

One of the most lucid, and pained, came from Schelling. Fastening onto the imputation that strategists were second-rate game theorists and that this accounted for their analytical style and foreign-policy premises, Schelling pointed out that of the seven strategists specifically named by Rapoport, only two—Herman Kahn and himself—had ever actually *used* game theory, and that Kahn's interest in it had only been "passing." Kissinger had never even been interested in it. On the other hand game theory had been extensively used by Rapoport himself and numerous writers in the "peace" camp, such as Kenneth Boulding.

Another review, which Rapoport subsequently said he "liked best of all the hostile reviews," was by D. G. Brennan, a member and former president of the Hudson Institute. Making the same point as Schelling, Brennan pointed out that in all the "reports, discussion papers and other documents" produced at the institute over the years—enough to fill perhaps twenty feet of shelf space—"the number of individual pages on which there is any discussion of concepts from game theory could be counted on one hand." He also picked on a passage in which Rapoport detected "a hypnotic obsession with the minimax 'solution'" in a statement by the British military writer, Sir Basil Liddell Hart, to the effect that tactical nuclear weapons, though a military liability to the West, could not be discarded because the Russians had also acquired them.

Brennan pointed out that Liddell Hart knew very little about game theory; in fact, on being shown Rapoport's paragraph, he had written to Brennan: "I have not made any close study of the new kind of games theory developed in America—and I find the jargon used by its exponents more puzzling than illuminating."

Yet both Brennan and Schelling accepted, in part, Rapoport's criticism of the narrowness and abstraction of much strategic thinking. Indeed Brennan wrote:

> Much of Rapoport's concern can probably be traced to a perception on the following lines: Strategists in general have focused more on aspects of international relations involving conflicting interests than on those aspects involving common interests, although a reasonable judge would hold that common interests greatly predominate. This distortion stems from preoccupation with oversimplified models in game theory, models that tend to channel thought into conflict-oriented grooves and away from perceptions of important common interests. This distortion of emphasis and values is communicated to larger publics via published writings of the strategists, in particular to political and military leaders who subconsciously assimilate it to their thoughts, policies and programs, thereby setting in motion a chain of events leading to responses from opponents that will ultimately change the reality into something more like the distortion.
>
> The only element in this perception that is wholly false is the ascription of the villainous role to game theory, an element that is not vital to the whole. . . .

In his reply to Brennan's review, published in the same issue (Vol. XXI, No. 10, Dec. 1965) of the *Bulletin of Atomic Scientists,* Rapoport said he accepted the foregoing as a very accurate statement of his main thesis—except on one vital point. The target of *Strategy and Conscience* had not been game theory but the use by strategists of oversimplified models of international relations. In fact, he had used game theory to show how misleading these models were.

> My main contention was that the strategists are under pressure to formulate decision problems on the "lower rungs of the decision problem ladder" (to borrow one of Mr. Kahn's metaphors). Those are the rungs where the choice of fundamental values seems more obvious and where the choice of criteria of rationality is not complicated by paradoxes. I at-

tribute the predominance of military-strategic considerations in American strategic literature to these pressures. In military strategy, tactics, and logistics, values can be more easily defined in terms of tangibles than in the realm of politics or of social welfare (let alone in realms where ethical issues loom). Also a military conflict can be more faithfully represented by a zero-sum paradigm than a social or ideological conflict. Again I must insist . . . that the knowledge of or use of game theory has nothing to do with this "pressure toward a zero-sum game formulation." By such pressure I mean a tendency to select for rigorous analysis precisely those situations which lend themselves most readily to such analysis. Where conflict between independent decision makers is involved, the situations which lend themselves most readily to rigorous analysis are those where the interests of the decision makers are diametrically opposed. Thus, even if there were no distortions (in the sense of assuming the interests to be diametrically opposed when in fact they are not), the *selection pressure* would bring most readily to the attention of the strategists those situations to which the zero-sum game paradigm applies, regardless of whether the strategists are versed in game theory or make use of its apparatus. Similarly, one need not be versed in formal logic in order to reason according to its precepts, nor need one know what "prose" means in order to speak prose.

11

WAR GAMES ON
THE CAMPUS

SINCE MODERN TECHNOLOGY has destroyed the exclusively
military character of war planning, and America's intercontinental missiles could to all intents be deployed, manned,
and operationally launched by the aerospace companies
which make them, it is not surprising to find many of the
techniques of military analysis being used in other fields.
This is the case with war games, which under various names
are widely employed for training and research in business
and the social sciences. Indeed business and the social sciences
have sometimes been ahead of the military in gaming.

Business gaming came into widespread use in the United
States in the early 1960s following the development of two
models. One—a manual game in which computations were
performed by "clerks" using desk calculators—was first described in 1958 by G. R. Andlinger and J. R. Greene in the
Harvard Business Review and subsequently became known

as the Harvard Business Review Game. (The materials and instructions were sold by the Review at $2 a set.) The other, using an IBM 650 computer, was developed in 1956 and after numerous test plays and modifications became part of the training course of the American Management Association at Saranac Lake, New York.

Both games have since inspired many others, and it is now almost mandatory for any advanced business school, or industrial or commercial corporation, to conduct games for management training or research.[1]

But the most noteworthy extension of the use of war games has been in the universities, particularly for the study of International Relations. One of the best-known models is the GENEX game, developed by Lincoln Bloomfield at M.I.T., which closely resembles the politico-military games played at the Pentagon. GENEX has provided the pattern for many other "crisis games" in universities in America and Europe. As I played in one of them—part of a series called CONEX —at Edinburgh University in 1967, I am tempted to describe it in some detail.

The CONEX model is a role-playing crisis game with a minimum of twenty roles and a maximum of thirty, exclud-

---

[1] In 1966 I watched the playing of an airline "war game" used regularly at the British Air Transport Staff College at East Burnham for training executives of BEA and BOAC. On this occasion it was being played by visiting teams from KLM, SAS, and Lufthansa. Each of the three companies started the game with identical conditions. Its fleet consisted of 10 jets and 20 turboprop airliners. A route network provided six stage lengths varying from 300 to 1,200 miles. There was a choice of six seating configurations for each type of aircraft; and seating arrangements and schedules could be geared to capture any or all of 48 possible types of travel market. Each team was told to organize itself round six functions: finance, purchasing, production, marketing, personnel and research, and general management. Costs were laid down for each operation (£3,000 for a 200-hour aircraft check, £200 for changing seating arrangements). Advantages could be gained by investing in nine possible types of market research, and the computer could throw a spanner into the works by creating, at random, a 14-day engineering strike. The game lasted 14 days and covered one financial year of simulated operations. Lufthansa, as I recall, had a slight edge on its competitors, with five months of operation still to go. A full account of the British airline game is contained in *Aeroplane,* October 6, 1966.

ing the Control team. It uses data based on the real world, but modified to play out a crisis some eighteen months in the future. It focuses on the Middle East and involves the Great Powers who feel they have an interest there. The nonaligned countries and the United Nations are also partly involved. The area is seen as embroiled in several crises at once, but the dominant one is the Arab-Israeli conflict which creates, among other things, an arms race.

In 1967 the scenario began with Egypt in a feverish state over the forthcoming opening of the Aswan Dam in the presence of Soviet leaders. Israel was equally excited over celebrating the twentieth anniversary of its foundation. It was also assumed to have major internal political problems and to have difficulty, largely for economic reasons, in matching the Arab states in conventional arms. The crisis was brought to a head by an Israeli appeal to America and France for nuclear support, failing which Israel threatened to "go nuclear" itself within a few months. Strong indications of this appeal were leaked, by a Control agent, to Egypt and Syria.

The game in which I participated (through a last-minute accident, as Israeli commander-in-chief) began pacifically enough, with government leaders on both sides recognizing the danger of war and seeking ways to avoid it. This aim was shared by the Great Powers, who helped to convene a United Nations General Assembly meeting. But arrangements broke down, partly as a result of local intrigues and partly because of growing suspicions among the Middle Eastern countries that their protectors were prepared to let them down in a general settlement. This was particularly true of Israel, to whom it appeared that if the Arabs attacked, the United States would not come to the rescue. (It also struck the Israeli commander that if Israel were to attack preemptively, the enemy could be defeated before United Nations or other intervention.) Accordingly a bargain was made with the opposition "war party" to overrule the Prime Minister; and when the game was terminated, after two and a half days' play, both sides were about to attack.

The game had a special interest six months later when, despite certain obvious differences in the scenario, Israel found itself in a similar predicament in the real world. Although it is axiomatic that politico-military games should never be used to predict real-world events, I am bound to confess that the "insight" that I had gained in this one convinced me that Israel had no choice but to preempt with an air strike at Egyptian concentrations in Sinai. This, of course, happened, and I have no doubt that had I been a policy maker, my temptation to predict from subsequent war games would have been strengthened.

The CONEX game, however, was not intended as a military, or even a political, exercise. The purpose of the series, organized by two social scientists and a psychologist, was simply to try out the method as a tool for research into human behavior in a crisis situation. For this reason it was accompanied by the filling in of numerous questionnaires by the participants about their personal attitudes before, during, and after the game.

A more typical game, from the standpoint of International Relations study, was a politico-military simulation at the University of Lancaster, described by a participant in the London *Financial Times* [2]:

> All of us devoted our weekend to being the guinea pig of Dr. Michael Nicholson, Senior Research Fellow of Conflict Studies at the university. Together with members of the academic staff, a few visitors like the Foreign Office men and undergraduates, we were divided into "countries"—Germany, Russia, France, Britain, Italy, the Austrian-Hungarian Empire (that was me), and Serbia.

[2] W. van der Eyken, "How I Saved Europe," *Financial Times*, London, April 19, 1967.

We all occupied different rooms in the university where we stayed for some ten hours, and we were all provided with a Civil Servant. Dr. Nicholson rather grandly announced that he was going to be God. Actually he called it Control, but we recognized that euphemism for the deity he really was. Each hour of our day represented a full day in the action of the crisis, and as the situation built up, those days were cut to half an hour each.

God's behaviour was typically Olympian. He began by announcing, perfectly accurately, that on March 21, 1909, Bülow, Head of the German Government, had written to Izvolsky, the Russian Foreign Minister, that Germany backed the Austrian-Hungarian annexation of Bosnia, which had occurred some time previously, and refused to bring pressure on Austria to attend a conference of Great Powers to discuss the seizure of territory.

This was a blow to Russia, which looked on the seizure as a threat to its own interests in the Balkans. One in the eye for Russia, we thought in our room. Hastily we wrote to our good friends the Germans, backing Bülow's move. Then we decided it might be quite fun and sense to try and isolate Russia still further from her treaty partners, France and Britain, and we wrote to Asquith making soothing noises and hoping, tongue in cheek, that they would join Austria in not making a major issue of what we assured them was a trifling local affair.

Messages between the rooms were leaping about now. Serbia was writing to Russia, we discovered later, seeking military support for what she rightly saw as a dire threat to her borders. France was trying to play a sort of "honest broker" role in the proceedings and Russia was staying rather ominously quiet. We could sense cordite in the air.

We were rather aggrieved about Italy. She was supposed to be part of the Great Alliance with Germany and Austria, but very soon began nagging about territories in the Tyrol which she claimed were hers, and we realized that she was not long for this particular partnership. God kept interfering. He sent scurrilous rumours of troop movements along the Danube scudding up and down the academic corridors, and at one time we found ourselves having to announce a military alert to combat them. This worried everyone, so we had to send more messages explaining that it was a defensive move and did not mean we were about to attack Serbia.

Then we had a brainwave. Let's start talking directly to Serbia and offer her a non-aggression pact, and in this way keep old Russia out of the Balkans. Secondly, let's make Control's life difficult by entering into communications with countries not included in the simulation, like Rumania and Bulgaria, and thus outflank Serbia and increase the pressure on that country so that they would be more inclined to make overtures. Drunk with power, we went even further and dispatched a message to Control asking our Chief-of-Police in Vienna to apprehend a dangerous trouble-maker called Adolf Schickelgruber, known to frequent beer cellars. If we could nip World War II in the bud as well, so much the better.

But Control beat us on this. "We have apprehended two men called Adolf Schickelgruber," read their reply. "The first, a dentist, was a dangerous element and has been taken in charge. But the second, a young house-painter, was clearly innocent and has been released." Such is the stuff of history. . . .

The writer goes on to describe how the game led ultimately to Italy's quitting the Triple Alliance and Austria-Hungary's obliging Serbia—over the fruit salad at Sunday lunch—to accept a nonaggression treaty. "And we set off to draft a joint communiqué to tell the world that the Bosnian Crisis was over."

Though the *Financial Times* account says little about the research aims of such crisis games (which we shall consider in a moment), it captures their spirit, from the player's point of view, very graphically.

From the goings-on at Lancaster, it is something of a letdown in excitement to describe the sober role playing which characterizes Inter-Nation Simulation (INS), an American game in which assessments are made by a computer in accordance with explicit rules. The principal exponent of INS is Professor Harold Guetzkow, of Northwestern University, Illinois. Guetzkow uses it for testing political hypotheses, and gives some typical examples: [3]

1. The longer decision-makers continue in office, the greater the tendency for similar decisions.
2. The longer decision-makers continue in office, the more constant others will expect their behavior to be.
3. The longer decision-makers continue in office, the greater is their adequacy in achieving their national goals in international affairs.

The conduct of INS resembles that of other "crisis games" in that the participants are grouped in national teams. But instead of representing "real" states, they inhabit imaginary ones with dull names like "Omnia" and "Dacia," [4] chosen to prevent emotional associations. Their roles, moreover, are not those of Prime Minister, Foreign Minister, etc., but those of a "central decision maker" (holding office), one or two "external decision makers" per team, and an "aspiring decision maker," who is out of office. There are five teams in the model, and each consists of three or four members.

The central decision maker performs the executive function of government. He maintains his position by satisfying imaginary elements of the population which "validate" his officeholding. The external decision makers represent the foreign relations structure of the nation, and are dependent on the central decision maker for continuance in office. In the simulation, these decision makers communicate directly with each other. The aspiring decision maker(s) represent leaders of "competing elites"—opposition parties, officer groups, financial interests, and so on.

[3] H. Guetzkow and others, *Simulation in International Relations* (Englewood Cliffs, N.J.: Prentice-Hall, Inc., 1963).
[4] S. A. Bornstein, "A Scenario Generation Methodology," prepared for SPAD Management Office DCS/Plans, HQ, Air Force Systems Cmd., Washington, D.C. (mimeo), Abt Associates, Inc., Cambridge, Mass., 1966.

An essential part of the game structure is the set of relations among actors *inside* each nation. The "validators," who exist only as an element of the computer program, derive satisfaction from two sources "each intended to represent a cluster of factors operating in the political, economic, and social life of the nation." These are (1) their consumption of goods and services, and (2) the nation's "force capability." From the basic capability of his simulated nation, given at the start, the central decision maker periodically makes short-term allocations to either. He may also plan for the long term by allocating basic resources to the generation of more basic capability, i.e., capital investment, which in turn may be used for future allocations. The opposing aspirant decision maker appeals to the same validators in the hope of getting into office.

The simulation allows for the fact that in some nations decision makers are politically very sensitive to deprivations imposed on their validators, while in others they have a great freedom. But in all cases the central decision maker may lose office to an aspiring decision maker who promises better to satisfy the validators' wants. This can happen either peacefully and legally, or through revolution.

Externally, nations are allowed to communicate with each other through their external decision makers; and direct bilateral communications may be supplemented by multilateral conferences. There is also a communication system external to the decision makers themselves, called a "world newspaper." This publishes statistical reports and news items based on its analysis of developments or derived from imaginary intelligence sources manipulated by Control.

As part of their international relationship, nations may trade their resources, either "raw" in the form of *basic capability units,* or "converted" in the form of *force capability units* or *consumption units.* They may also make grants of aid to other nations. Alliances may be formed. International organizations can be set up. And resort may be had to war.

Although the highly simplified nature of the simulation makes the consequences of participants' decisions generally predictable, unexpected developments can occur through the occasional use of Monte Carlo-type techniques in the computing process, or as a result of decision makers adopting an unusual strategy.

The model, it is claimed, "reproduces important features of international relations processes" so that "decision makers work within a conceptual environment similar to the decision-environment confronted by members of governments." [5]

INS is played in 75-minute time periods. At the start of each period the participants receive a sheet of paper giving their initial capabilities or the results for their nation of the previous period's decision, worked out by the computer. The remainder of the sheet is for entering decisions taken during the move. These are expressed numerically in the form of units allocated to the generation of new basic capability, units allocated to consumption satisfaction, consumption units imported or exported, and so on.

An essential part of the simulation is a series of scales. For example there is an 11-point scale for measuring the satisfaction of the validators, who, as we have seen, exist only conceptually. There is also a 10-point scale for measuring the "decision latitude" of the central decision maker, i.e., his ability to disregard the dissatisfaction of the validators with impunity. Changes in decision latitude are determined by the validators operating under Control. A central decision maker may recognize such changes or oppose them. But if he opposes them, the resulting disturbance in the national political system is registered as a decrease in the basic capability of the nation, including, of course, its force capability for defense or attack. There is also an 11-point scale for the probability of officeholding. If at the end of any time period

[5] Guetzkow, *op. cit.*

the overall "validator satisfaction" drops below a so-called revolution threshold, a Monte Carlo device is used by the researcher to decide whether a revolution takes place. If it does, a second Monte Carlo decision is made as to whether it succeeds, in which case the central decision maker is changed. But whether it suceeds or not, a revolution is put down as a cost to the nation, generally about 20 percent of its basic capability units.

The rules for war are slightly more elaborate. It may occur by declaration at any time and the attackers must record the proportion of force capability allocated. The target nation must respond, after consulting its allies, within fifteen minutes. If there is no surrender, the nation's decision makers must state the force capability they are committing to defense or retaliation, and the experimenter calculates and announces each side's probability of victory. During the next fifteen minutes, the belligerents may (a) negotiate a truce, (b) agree to a "decisive battle" whose outcome is determined by the announced probability of victory in conjunction with random numbers, or (c) continue the war by allocating additional capabilities. If (c) occurs, the procedure is repeated until (a) or (b) happens.

This partial explanation may give some idea of how INS works, though in fairness the student is advised to read Guetzkow's book.

When I met Guetzkow on the Northwestern campus, by the shore of Lake Michigan, he told me he had come into the simulation business as a social psychologist. He recalled that back in the 1930s experimental psychologists and sociologists had developed the use of face-to-face groups in laboratories to test theories of group reactions. This work had been elaborated in the laboratory study of organizations with component parts, particularly at the Carnegie Institute of Technology, where he was working in the Graduate School of Industrial Administration after World War II (in which he had been a conscientious objector). The use of face-to-face groups in group organization study had led him to consider a further step in the study of social systems—the contriving of an *interorganizational* system.

Two other developments had inspired him. One was the work of Richard Snyder (now codirector of Northwestern's International Relations program on decision making in public administration. The other was Goldhamer's work on political games at Rand. Out of these came his development of INS, which was "a real simulation, whereas face-to-face groups, even in a laboratory, are more replications of reality than simulations."

Guetzkow began work on INS in 1957 with a grant from the Carnegie Corporation. The first runs were manual, with only an adding machine to help calculations. Then a grant came from the Air Force Office of Scientific Research. Next, funds were provided under a program called Project Michaelson for a run at the Naval Ordnance Test Station at China Lake. This included a simulation of the historically recorded events which took place in the six weeks before the outbreak of World War I. Finally the Advanced Research Projects Agency, which sponsored Abt's AGILE guerrilla warfare game, provided funds up to 1969.

Guetzkow said he believed INS would prove its value in clarifying our theories of international relations. Although it was only *one* way of making models of social systems, it called for clearer formulation than others generally did. To use it, he said, one had to be precise in specifying variables and the interlocking relationship between them. This was necessary to provide the decision makers with "feedback," i.e., immediate knowledge of the consequence of their actions. Eventually, he thought, it would be necessary to appraise the personal style and presuppositions of decision makers, so as to study their influence on events. Ultimately it might even be possible to compute not only the consequences of decisions, but the player's calculations of these consequences as well. But Guetzkow thought it would take another century or two to develop a comprehensive computer model of international relations processes with which to predict the course of international relations themselves.

Despite Guetzkow's distant perspective, one or two full computer models of international relations processes have in fact been tried out. TEMPER (see page 156) was one of them. Another is the "Simple Diplomatic Game" developed by Oliver Benson at the University of Oklahoma.[6] In this the model consists of two sets of variables—"action variables" and "situation variables"—and a program specifying the relationship between variables and outcomes. The action variables consist of nine possible acting nations, nine possible target nations, and nine possible "intensity levels" of action. The last range through

> .100 diplomatic protest
> .200 United Nations action
> .300 severing diplomatic relations
> .400 propaganda-subversion campaign
> .500 boycott and/or reprisals
> .600 troop movements
> .700 full mobilization
> .800 limited war
> .900 all-out war.

The nine actor nations in the model are the United States, Britain, the Soviet Union, West Germany, France, Italy, India, China, and Japan. The nine target states are Korea, Guatemala, Egypt, Lebanon, Hungary, Vietnam, Taiwan, Indonesia, and Iran.

The situation variables describe the "state of the system" at any given moment. They are (1) national power expressed in terms of war potential, (2) distribution of this power, (3) the degree of involvement of one state with another, and (4)

6 O. Benson, "A Simple Diplomatic Game—or Putting One and One Together" (mimeo) (Norman: University of Oklahoma, 1959).

the propensity to act, or counteract, of each state. The involvement index is based on the amount of mutual trade between nations, coalition membership, the presence or absence of foreign military bases in a target area, and geographic proximity. Propensity to act is based on data suggested by Quincy Wright's voluminous *A Study of War*.

Political simulation games are extolled by their exponents as a form of experimentation on a variety of grounds. It is said, for example, that scientific data on international relations are hard to obtain; that situations likely to occur in the future may never have happened in the past; that, despite the abundance of diplomatic history, the same event seldom "happens twice"; that events in a simulation are easily observed; and that these events and the factors determining them can be manipulated by the researcher. But when all is said and done, the exponents of simulation (both civil and military) use a form of experimentation which is very different from the experimentation practiced by the physical scientist using real materials.

We have seen the danger of the method in the military field: namely that quasi-experimentation yields quasi-answers, and that while these may have a limited usefulness, for example in leading one to consider possibilities that might not otherwise have been suggested, they may also come to be taken for *real* answers. In academic research a similar danger may exist. For while the purpose of simulation is generally given as "heuristic," i.e., valuable for stimulating empirical research but incapable of providing proof, its ultimate and unacknowledged purpose often looks like being the subjection of hypotheses to a *test*.

The argument *against* the use of simulation techniques was put to me by David Singer, a Research Political Scientist of the Mental Health Research Institute, at the University of Michigan, whom I was recommended to see, with academic broad-mindedness, by Guetzkow. Singer has emphatic ideas on the pitfalls of simulation, which he imparts to visitors as he takes them on the pillion of his motorbike around the Ann Arbor campus.

Guetzkow, he said, had the best simulation method. "But when we're short of men and money, we have to give priorities in the allocation of resources. Simulation just isn't value for money." The simulators went to great trouble and expense to construct models for reproducing certain characteristics of the "real world" in the laboratory—and then spent their time simulating everything from the Congress of Vienna onwards in an effort to see if the model, when played, produced anything like "real history."

"Why not go and analyze the real world directly?" he asked.

The simulators, said Singer, worked on the assumption that the world of politics and strategy was not open to accurate analysis. To some extent one could understand their point. The social sciences, particularly in the study of international relations, were terribly short of data. "Data," he said, "are not just facts. They are facts that have been converted into a form suitable for scientific purposes, which means they have to go through a kind of screen." He cited the case of official statistics which, unless obviously tampered with by governments, might seem to be data par excellence. But even statistics might be terribly partial, and had to be supplemented by other information before they could be used scientifically.

In the case of the "raw material" of history—diaries, memoirs, diplomatic documents, and so on—data-making was a very arduous task. The writers often included only what they wanted, and even the most conscientiously objective document was selective. But it was wrong to suppose that data could be made more easily and reliably in a laboratory model, which in any case could not be constructed without some *real world* data. These data were then "weighted" or subjected to probabilistic processes that could vitiate the whole model.

The alternative, Singer said, was the method of content

analysis, which was being developed for International Relations research at Stanford University. This involved coding, classifying, and quantifying the key variants in international relations. When you had done this, you had a means whereby almost any research worker could assess and sort the facts. One method of doing it was by analyzing the "perceptual variables" in the material, which included the relationship of the perceiver to what he perceived. The Stanford University project had concentrated on material relating to the period immediately before World War I, and on material about the contemporary Sino-Soviet crisis. But other content analysis projects had been concerned with different and equally important variables, such as behavioral ones.

Singer took up Guetzkow's claim that internation simulation obliged one to be precise in one's specification of variables and their "interlocking" relationship. That was a fine and necessary thing, he said. It would be good if every researcher treated variables and their interrelationship as if they were going to be put on IBM punched cards. But there was no need to go on and actually *simulate* them.

He also contested the claim of the simulators, Guetzkow and Snyder, that simulation was useful for generating hypotheses. He thought many of the hypotheses being examined by the simulators had been thought of long before the latter went in for simulation. "In any case," he said, "the researcher will hardly have more or better hypotheses suggested to him by following the activities of a dozen or so students acting as decision makers of imaginary nations than by (a) reading history, (b) studying the research literature in this or that analogous or related field, or (c) just imagining.

"In fact," he added, "a good deal of expensive and time-consuming social science research which the researchers claim has a 'heuristic value' is of little more value than just plain thinking—and occasionally of much less."

The other claim made by the simulators, said Singer, was

that they were able to control and *manipulate* their material; in other words, that they were nearer to their empirical world. It was true, he admitted, that the social science researcher never worked directly with reality. The diplomat's phrase, the aide-de-camp's minutes, were only a *representation* of the event they described; and data-making processes such as content analysis took one yet further away from the real thing. "But the question is whether the greater susceptibility of *simulated* facts to useful data-making compensates the distortion that occurs in converting the 'real world' into a model. I don't think so. Even though the researcher in simulation—man, man-machine, or machine—is closer to his empirical world than is the user of historical evidence, the simulated world will be too unlike the real world to be valid enough for ever verifying hypotheses."

To myself, as an outsider to the controversy over the use of simulation techniques in social science research, Singer's arguments seemed cogent. But I was also reminded that there is a practical difference between social science simulation exercises whose results go into the mill of academic criticism, and secret military war games whose results and "lessons" are liable to show up with terrible suddenness in new defense postures, new weapons, new contingency plans, and ventures like Vietnam.

Moreover, since International Relations covers a fairly broad range of human activity, the use of simulation in its study might at least be expected to produce a fuller and more balanced selection of ideas (even if these could not be tested) than simulation exercises in the narrow field of defense.

My chief impression from what I saw of the nonmilitary side of war gaming—"peace gaming" might be the way some exponents would describe it—was of the size of the problems it was trying to overcome, and the crudity of its methods. If the social scientists were so clearly at the very beginning of the road—for example in data-making—how long would it take them, I wondered, to uncover the causes of those wars which the military researchers, with equally questionable optimism, were seeking to make sure that we would win?

12

VIETNAM—THE GAME
THAT FAILED

WE HAVE TRACED the development of war games from their first beginning to the current "state of the art." Collectively they represent a vast investment of time, ingenuity, and money. But how have they served us?

The answer to this question will be partly determined by the moral beliefs of the questioner. If he is a pacifist, he will say that any technique which sets out to advise the military planner, however imperfectly, is against the human good. But there may be others who have read this far who, while recognizing the moral and military impasse to which thermonuclear weapons have brought us, still hesitate to say that the use of arms is to be condemned in all circumstances. These will be logically bound to consider the question from the military-technical standpoint.

If we look at the period from the nineteenth century up to 1918—what might be called the amateur age of gaming—the record was inauspicious. (Though where war-game lessons were modestly applied, as in the British war game of 1905, they successfully served a military purpose.) The Japanese naval games were really an extension of the amateur age, and brought a terrible retribution on their users.

Generally, World War II brought a more careful way of doing things, but the success of operational research was only made possible by the availability of actual battle experience, and—perhaps one should add—by the realism of the scientists engaged in it, who understood what quantitative analysis could treat and what it could not.

Thermonuclear weapons brought an entirely new situation in which operational research, in the accepted sense, was impossible; because no amount of research could give a scientific answer about the total effect of such weapons in a war. But the demand of soldiers and statesmen for some answer, however crude, to help them in their difficulties was immensely strong.

In the early days, before both superpowers had such large nuclear stockpiles as now, this demand arose from the necessity of telling oneself, and then the world, that one had a capability to "take out" a critically large number of targets. (At this stage it was the enemy's cities.) Later, when the deterrent threat of an all-out nuclear blow became incredible, it became necessary to convince oneself and the world that nuclear war could be fought within limits. (The targets then became the enemy's missile sites, though the "hardening" of missile sites has now caused them to become cities again.)

In all this, war games and associated forms of analysis offered an indispensable means of bolstering the hopes and assertions of the national leaders, and also of justifying to the electorate the vast sums of money spent on hardware. In fact, if war games had not been adopted in the concurrent effort to decide how to apportion resources among competing projects, it would almost certainly have been necessary to invent them for propaganda purposes.

But, in fact, the trouble went deeper than that. For the techniques adopted to rationalize existing policies gradually came to be accepted as guides in the selection of new ones; or, to put it more accurately, the uncertain assumptions on which all war-game solutions were based became forgotten. To see that this happened it is only necessary to look at the example of war games on conventional or "sub-conventional" war—the kind of war fought in Vietnam.

Almost from the outset, Vietnam has been the fullest gamed, fullest analyzed, and most intensively "planned" war in history. It may not have been *literally* planned by computer. (To my knowledge, no operational decisions have yet been taken on the basis of computer games like AGILE.) But all the neat concepts of the computer gamers are directly interchangeable with those taught at U.S. Army and Special Forces schools. Its air war tactics have been repeatedly gamed by the Air Force, which in the past five years has lost more than 2,000 aircraft, about 40 percent of them in accidents or through enemy action on the ground—a contingency the designers of AFWET were not asked to envisage. The biggest failure, however, has been in the higher echelons, where numerous aspects of today's war in Vietnam, and tomorrow's in Thailand, have been gamed in Pentagon politico-military games over five or six years.

Indeed, it might not be pressing the point too hard to say that the prestige of war games, and the analytical methods associated with them, has itself become an element in the war. For certainly the war—still in progress as this is written —has long ceased to be primarily a struggle to preserve the Republic of Vietnam, or even Southeast Asia. It has become, rather, an all-out effort to vindicate the reputation of the American military machine, not only the quality of its soldiers and the efficacy of its firepower but also, and above all, the worth of its military assessments.

And the most salient of these assessments, as anyone who has visited its headquarters and field commands knows, has been that the enemy in Vietnam can be defeated by fire-power, air mobility, and rural pacification.

If American military judgment is proved wrong on this point—and it seems to have been so proved for some time now—the repercussions will extend far beyond Southeast Asia. In particular they will reach Europe, where the whole concept of Atlantic collective security, based on the United States nuclear guarantee and the token presence of American forces in Germany, is already much questioned. The weakening of NATO was always foreseeable because of changes in the strategic nuclear context and the recession of an immediate threat. But nobody could have foreseen, even a few years ago, the total collapse of America's moral authority in Europe as a result of military and political blunders in Asia.

War games bear a major share of responsibility for these blunders, and their part in them cannot be dismissed by saying that it is impossible to link war game analyses with particular policy decisions. Firstly, this is not quite true. For example, the 1962 decision to cancel Skybolt, which had such far-reaching political consequences in Europe, was the direct result of computer games. Secondly, it is not necessary to be able to quantify the influence of a factor in order to know that it exists. (The computer itself has already led to the disregard of too many factors in American policy making simply because they cannot be quantified and it cannot assimilate them.) War games have in fact become deeply entwined with policy making, not so much by prescribing solutions as by leading to the making of the particularly narrow "quantifiable" type of policy decision that war games can be used to evaluate and test.

Now, those who have used or misused war games bear a heavy blame. But so long as military means are necessary to national security, it would be ridiculous to dismiss the importance of military analysis properly applied. It is necessary to be clear on this point. For no one questions the use of computer games to discover an optimum gun caliber, or the costs of a weapons system, or the measurable aspects of its performance. The need is to recognize their limitations, the number of factors they necessarily require, and the importance of the area where judgments have to be made on the fallible basis of intuition. A similar point must be made about politico-military games intended to improve judgment. We have seen their pitfalls. But obviously a well-run game could encourage policy makers to think more flexibly if it examined the whole basis of an existing policy and not just a variety of tactical alternatives for seeking the same end.

Put this way, the method of correcting war-game errors which have entered into American defense planning might seem relatively straightforward, if not particularly easy in practice. It would amount to telling the policy makers, as one would a commander in battle: "Examine all the alternatives; remember the limits of the data; then act in the light of your judgment." But in peacetime defense planning (if the phrase may still be used) a higher kind of judgment is needed. This concerns the fallibility of one's technical judgment. For whereas in a battle the commander who doubts his own judgment is lost, it could be said without a paradox that in peacetime defense planning we suffer not from too many doubts but from too few.

If we accept this proposition, which the American experience in Vietnam seems to reinforce, the debate about war games ceases to be military-technical. For if military planning is so open to error, ought we not to pay more attention to alternative forms of planning for national and international security? In fact, some of the alternatives might lend themselves more reliably, and less dangerously, to analytical techniques such as this book has described.

To understand what I am here suggesting, it is necessary to digress briefly and examine what "defense" really means. The concept of defense has been broadened by modern governments to include many things not formerly envisaged by it.

At one end of the scale it embraces policies of nuclear deterrence; at the other the pursuit, by military means, of foreign policy objectives whose relationship to defense is often hard to discern. Many people may feel that the latter extension is responsible for most of our present troubles. Yet within the arguments frequently used by the Great Powers to rationalize foreign policy adventures there is a kernel of truth. Modern technology, by increasing the ranges of weapons and the speed of communications, has so shrunk the world that distant events which might once have been regarded as none of a nation's business are now often of more immediate (and legitimate) concern to it than those closer at hand. Global "peacekeeping," though an overworked phrase, is not necessarily a dishonest one.

But where do the threats to peace lie? This is a crucial question, which in turn must lead us to ask another: Is defense, after all, still too *narrowly* defined—and have those extensions given it been the right ones?

Much has been written about the threat posed to human existence by modern weapons, not all of which are nuclear. But dangerous as they may be, it is not the weapons themselves that threaten peace, but the moral, psychological, political, social, and economic conditions which have led to their acquisition and could lead to their use. It is, therefore, these conditions which will have to be changed if peace is to come nearer. But this does not mean that they *will* be changed, or that the opportunities to change them are anything but limited.

When one examines the moral condition of mankind, one would like to believe, with Professor Rapoport, that "conscience" offers a means of escape from the international Prisoner's Dilemma game. But although one might share his philosophy, one would have difficulty in finding evidence of the general support necessary to make it work. Christianity has been preaching it for two thousand years, and Buddhism even longer, but they have not prevented our present impasse.

It may well be that, given time, psychological research will uncover the reasons why they have failed, and that armed with this knowledge we can set about constructing a safer political and social system. But psychological research is acknowledged to be in its infancy, and in the long term, as Keynes observed in a less macabre context, we shall all be dead. Similarly gloomy observations can be made about political research directed toward finding a new theory of international relations as an alternative to accepted balance-of-power theories. But this is not to disparage such research. On the contrary, the shortness of time that may separate us from nuclear war (and almost certainly separates us from the next major "limited" war) might be seen as an argument for giving such research more support. Certainly there is a perversity about our system of priorities which allots so much effort to military research and so little to finding ways and means of preventing war at its roots.

In these researches simulation, the cousin of war gaming, may yet have a place. Though the cautions which apply to war gaming must apply to peace gaming as well.

But the most tractable field for peace research, or perhaps one should say peacekeeping research, is surely the economic. For here one is dealing, as one is not in the others, with factors that are measurable. Not only are the methods of economic research further advanced than those of the other social sciences, but some of the war-game techniques now applied in the defense field have already been practiced in the economic more successfully.

What I am suggesting, then, is that "defense" should be redefined to cover other threats to peace than the military one. There is nothing academic or abstract about some of these threats. In fact, the advance of a world famine can be timed on the basis of current statistics with a precision that no military calculation can bear. Many would think that it presents a graver problem than the risk of nuclear war.

I am also suggesting that research into methods of meeting

such threats would produce surer results than much current military research—in fact, that the research effort itself would be more cost-effective.

Now, of course, the notion of promoting national and international security through various forms of assistance is not new. It has been practiced regularly since the end of World War II, as a manifestation of alliance politics and to a lesser extent through contributions to United Nations programs. But the granting of such aid has been haphazard, and its volume in proportion to defense expenditure has been meager. For example, in 1967 the United States spent $1,900 million on nonmilitary aid programs (a quarter of one percent of the Gross National Product), compared with $73,000 million on Defense (9.2 percent of the GNP). The United Kingdom ratio was slightly more generous—about one half of one percent of the GNP on overseas development aid (about $580 million), compared with 6.5 percent ($6,200 million) on Defense. Many West European countries spent proportionately *less* on civil aid programs.

Although such grants of aid are naturally scrutinized by governments in relation to the results they may achieve, no attempt is currently made in any Western country to assess the peacekeeping effectiveness of various types of development assistance program. Nor is any attempt made to weigh up the effectiveness of aid budgets compared with military budgets—let alone to weigh up a particular aid program in comparison with a particular defense project, for example the cost-benefits of building a railway in Central Africa compared with those of maintaining a squadron of combat aircraft for a given period.

To give this example, is, of course, to illustrate the complexity of the task. But it is unlikely to be more formidable than comparing, say, the cost-effectiveness of a squadron of combat aircraft for brush-fire war with that of a squadron of frigates for antisubmarine warfare in the Atlantic. Parts of the operation will be quantifiable; others will require judgment and the analysis of other factors. But at least the results of the civil operation will be more open to monitoring—and mistakes, in both operation and analysis, may be more quickly identifiable.

The first step to such a procedure would be to put both military and nonmilitary budgets on an "input-out" basis, showing both the cost of each item and its expected returns described in an intelligible way. The second would be to end the budgetary competition between military spending departments and those concerned with the broader aspects of security by creating, in each country, a department or committee responsible for analyzing the operations of both. Such a reorganization would be bitterly contested by the military-industrial complex. But when one considers the threats to peace arising from such things as world hunger, the growing technological gap between poor and rich nations, and the resentment of primary producing countries of others' control of commodity market, it would surely not be too radical a step. Indeed, if Defense is defined as circumstances now dictate, it would be no more radical than the amalgamation, now generally accepted, of the budgetary claims of competing military services.

Here, then, is a task to which some of the skills which go into Defense research could usefully be applied.

I make no apology for ending this book on a personal note. In the course of a visit to the United States while writing it, I found myself one evening on the cliffs at Santa Monica, where I had just spent three days talking with war-game experts at the Rand Corporation. They had all been very courteous as well as very intelligent men and had readily discussed the "contras" of my subject as well as the "pros." Watching the sun set across the Pacific I asked myself conscientiously whether the conclusions I had begun to form about current trends in military analysis were not too harsh; and whether I was not doing an injustice to the wisdom of the American strategic establishment. I remember calculating, as the sun touched the horizon, that by looking a few degrees left of it, I could look across the ocean towards Saigon. Could one be so sure, I asked myself, that the American military planning apparatus might not in the end be vindicated, even in Southeast Asia?

Seven weeks later, during one of those breaks in writing which I fear may be too clearly reflected in the foregoing pages, I found myself on operations with the U.S. Marines near the Vietnam Demilitarized Zone. In now different circumstances, watching the parachute flares sink down on the sad hillsides, I asked myself the same question again. I was seeing, not for the first time, the lessons of war games applied in action—and some, I had to admit, had been well and profitably learned. The logistic apparatus in Vietnam was superlative. I had seen operations by the Air Cavalry that were as perfect in execution as a battle school firepower demonstration. Tactically, at that stage of the war anyway, the running was being made by the American forces.

It was only when one looked at the toll of civilian casualties, the impoverishment of the countryside, the growing refugee problem, the degradation and demoralization of Saigon, that one saw the extent of the moral and strategic trap into which America had fallen—a trap from which even "victory" could never rescue it. Here were the factors with which no war game had reckoned, or perhaps could *ever* properly reckon. The consequences of overlooking them—the cost in life and treasure, the loss of allies, the exposure of military impotence, the effects on American national unity and the American character—would reach out in ever-increasing circles for years to come.

INDEX

Index of Names

Index of Games

217

INVENTORY '80